Sport Heritage

Sport has become an important avenue in how we interpret, remember and maintain our heritage. Whether it is being applied in tourism marketing and development, employed as a vehicle for social cohesion or utilized as a way of articulating personal and collective identities, sport heritage is a vital topic in understanding what we value about the sporting past now, and what we wish to pass on to future generations. This edited collection brings together many new and exciting international approaches to sport heritage. Each of the chapters in this collection provides a thought-provoking sport heritage case study that would be of interest to students and researchers in history, geography, anthropology and marketing, as well as industry practitioners working at sporting events, at sports-based heritage attractions such as museums and halls of fame and at sports stadia and facilities. In addition, this collection would be of interest to those readers with a more general interest in sport heritage and the sporting past.

This book was originally published as a special issue of the *Journal of Heritage Tourism*.

Gregory Ramshaw is based at the Department of Parks, Recreation and Tourism Management at Clemson University, South Carolina. He explores the social construction and cultural production of heritage, with a particular interest in sport-based heritage. He is also the co-editor of *Heritage Sport Heritage: Sporting Pasts – Tourist Futures* and *Heritage and the Olympics: People, Place and Performance*, both published by Routledge.

Sport Heritage

Edited by
Gregory Ramshaw

Routledge
Taylor & Francis Group

LONDON AND NEW YORK

First published 2015
by Routledge

2 Park Square, Milton Park, Abingdon, Oxon OX14 4RN
711 Third Avenue, New York, NY 10017, USA

Routledge is an imprint of the Taylor & Francis Group, an informa business

First issued in paperback 2017

British Library Cataloguing in Publication Data
A catalogue record for this book is available from the British Library

ISBN 13: 978-1-138-84488-9 (hbk)
ISBN 13: 978-1-138-05716-6 (pbk)

Typeset in Times New Roman
by RefineCatch Limited, Bungay, Suffolk

Publisher's Note
The publisher accepts responsibility for any inconsistencies that may have
arisen during the conversion of this book from journal articles to book chapters,
namely the possible inclusion of journal terminology.

Disclaimer
Every effort has been made to contact copyright holders for their permission to
reprint material in this book. The publishers would be grateful to hear from any
copyright holder who is not here acknowledged and will undertake to rectify
any errors or omissions in future editions of this book.

Contents

Citation Information

The chapters in this book were originally published in the *Journal of Heritage Tourism*, volume 9, issue 3 (August 2014). When citing this material, please use the original page numbering for each article, as follows:

Chapter 1

Editorial: Sport, heritage, and tourism
Gregory Ramshaw
Journal of Heritage Tourism, volume 9, issue 3 (August 2014) pp. 191–196

Chapter 2

It still goes on: football and the heritage of the Great War in Britain
Ross J. Wilson
Journal of Heritage Tourism, volume 9, issue 3 (August 2014) pp. 197–211

Chapter 3

Indigenous sport and heritage: Cherbourg's Ration Shed Museum
Murray G. Phillips, Gary Osmond and Sandra Morgan
Journal of Heritage Tourism, volume 9, issue 3 (August 2014) pp. 212–227

Chapter 4

Identity in the "Road Racing Capital of the World": heritage, geography and contested spaces
Ray Moore, Matthew Richardson and Claire Corkill
Journal of Heritage Tourism, volume 9, issue 3 (August 2014) pp. 228–245

Chapter 5

Heroes as heritage: the commoditization of sporting achievement
Sean J. Gammon
Journal of Heritage Tourism, volume 9, issue 3 (August 2014) pp. 246–256

Chapter 6

A Canterbury tale: imaginative genealogies and existential heritage tourism at the St. Lawrence Ground
Gregory Ramshaw
Journal of Heritage Tourism, volume 9, issue 3 (August 2014) pp. 257–269

Please direct any queries you may have about the citations to
clsuk.permissions@cengage.com

Notes on Contributors

Claire Corkill is a research student at the University of York. She has recently completed a PhD which focused on the First World War Internment Camp at Knockaloe on the Isle of Man, which used digital technologies to reconstruct the various narratives of the camp. Claire's interest in the Isle of Man's racing heritage has developed from a family background that is ingrained within the events history.

Sean J. Gammon is based in the School of Sport, Tourism and the Outdoors at The University of Central Lancashire. He is widely published in the area of sport tourism, primarily focusing upon motivation, nostalgia and heritage. In addition he continues to contribute to the field of leisure, recently co-editing (with Sam Elkington) a new text on *Landscapes in Leisure: Space, Place and Identities*.

Ray Moore is a digital archivist at the University of York. His doctoral thesis examined the medieval settlement of the Isle of Man, using a web-based platform to explore the role of the past in the expression of contemporary narratives and identities. Ray's work continues to explore the role that the contemporary landscape can take in the expression of national, local and personal identities.

Sandra Morgan is an Aboriginal Elder from Cherbourg, Queensland. As chairperson of the Ration Shed Museum and president of the Historical Heritage Precinct Group, she has been instrumental in preserving Cherbourg's history.

Gary Osmond is Senior Lecturer in Sport History in the School of Human Movement Studies at The University of Queensland. His research interests include race and sport, as well as material, visual and digital representations of sport history. His most recent book is Gary Osmond and Murray G. Phillips (eds) *Sport History in the Digital Era* (2015).

Murray G. Phillips is Associate Professor in the School of Human Movement Studies at The University of Queensland. He has written on the historical aspects of several sports, including swimming and the Paralympics, as well as contributing to philosophical debates about sport history, understanding the role of sport museums and conceptualizing changes to sport history in the digital age. His most recent books are *Representing the Sporting Past in Museums and Halls of Fame* (2012) and Richard Pringle and Murray G. Phillips (eds) *Critical Sport Histories: Paradigms, Politics and the Postmodern Turn* (2013).

Gregory Ramshaw is based at the Department of Parks, Recreation and Tourism Management at Clemson University, South Carolina. He explores the social construction and cultural production of heritage, with a particular interest in sport-based heritage.

He is also the co-editor of *Heritage Sport and Tourism: Sporting Pasts – Tourist Futures* and *Heritage and the Olympics: People, Place and Performance*, both published by Routledge.

Matthew Richardson is Curator of Social History at Manx National Heritage. He is responsible for the care and interpretation of a wide-ranging collection representing all aspects of the history of the Isle of Man, from the seventeenth century to the present day. He is particularly interested in the Island's motorcycle racing heritage, and has put together a number of temporary exhibitions on this subject in recent years.

Ross J. Wilson is Senior Lecturer in Modern History and Public Heritage at the University of Chichester. He has written on the experience, representation and memory of the First World War in Britain and the United States. His wider research focuses on issues of museum, media and heritage representations in the modern era. This work has been published in the books *Representing Enslavement and Abolition in Museums* (2011), *Landscapes of the Western Front* (2012), *Cultural Heritage of the Great War in Britain* (2013) and *New York in the Great War* (2014).

Sport, heritage, and tourism

Gregory Ramshaw

Department of Parks, Recreation & Tourism Management, Clemson University, Clemson, SC, USA

The relationship between sport, heritage, and tourism is strong, and the breadth and depth of research that explores this relationship is significant. This collection adds to the heritage sport tourism literature by considering several new perspectives. In particular, authors have examined sport heritage as a vehicle for understanding and memorializing conflict, as a tool for both celebrating achievement and marginalizing people, as a field of dissonance that often does not conform to tourism promotion and marketing, as a topic that generates, commends, commodifies, and (sometimes) discards "living" heritage, and as a means for discovering, or imagining, genealogical roots. Ultimately, sport heritage illuminates many of the issues, challenges, and debates in heritage and heritage tourism more broadly, while also demonstrating that, through its constant making remaking, sport heritage rarely fossilizes.

There exists a strong connection between sport, heritage, and tourism. Sport can be seen as a window into peoples' culture (MacGregor, 2006; Timothy, 2011) while cultural travellers have long journeyed for sport-related purposes (Higham & Hinch, 2009; Hinch & Higham, 2011). As such, sport-based travel can be viewed through the lens of heritage (Ramshaw & Gammon, 2005). Sport halls of fame and museums, for example, have been examined as to their role in creating and disseminating the sporting past (Adair, 2004; Kidd, 1996; Redmond, 1973; Snyder, 1991; Springwood, 1996; Vamplew, 1998) and their relationship to broader social, political, and economic agendas (Cronin, 2012; Ramshaw, 2010). Sports stadia and sporting venues have been explored as potential tourist attractions (Friedman, 2007; Gammon, 2011; John, Sheard, & Vickery, 2007; Leask & Digance, 2002), their relationship in commodifying memory (Wright, 2012), their role in creating authentic experiences (Gammon & Fear, 2007; Ramshaw, Gammon, & Huang, 2013), and their part in constructing national identities (Ramshaw & Gammon, 2010). Heritage-based sporting events have been explored as avenues for maintaining expressions of cultural identity (Hinch & de la Barre, 2005; Hinch & Ramshaw, 2014), as creators of heritage-based place identities (Ramshaw & Hinch, 2006), as reflectors of heritage dissonance (Brittain, Ramshaw, & Gammon, 2013; Schultz, 2012; Smith, 2012; White, 2013), as promoters of non-sport heritage (Boukas, Ziakas, & Boustras, 2013), and as constructors of liminal heritages (Anton, Garrett, Hess, Miles, & Moreau, 2013). Sport heritage also has been positioned as a form of secular pilgrimage (Gammon, 2004; Williams, 2012), as a catalyst for diasporic travel (Joseph, 2011), and as an avenue for memorialization (McGuinness, 2012). Sport heritage has further been explored as to its unique management and conservation issues (Strohmayer, 2013; Titterington & Done, 2012; Vamplew, 2012), its relationship to sport history (Hill, 2012; O'Neill & Osmond, 2012; Phillips, 2012), and its role in creating intangible legacies (Day, Carter, & Carpenter, 2013). The broad base of interdisciplinary research that has examined sport heritage, particularly in a relatively short period of time, demonstrates the powerful role sport plays in our understanding of heritage and heritage tourism.

This collection builds upon this growing sport heritage literature by considering several new ways, to view the sport, heritage, and tourism landscape. However, these perspectives need not just be about sport and sport heritage, rather they also confront many of the broader issues addressed in heritage studies and heritage tourism. Consider Wilson's examination of the role of football in the memorialization of the First World War, a prescient topic given the numerous centenary commemorations occurring between 2014 and 2018. Certainly, sport played a role in the First World War, from the many athletes and administrators who fought in the War through to the now infamous Christmas Truce football matches, but it is the way that sport – and, football in particular – is used as a lens for remembering the War and for commemorating and memorializing the conflict that is of broader interest to heritage scholars. Football, Wilson argues, provides an emotive bridge as well as a marker for many British tourists. However, the emphasis on football also reveals much about contemporary British culture, as well as how the War is understood and remembered in Britain today. As such, this paper confronts many of the issues at play in contemporary heritage literature, albeit through a sports lens, including contestation over memory and memorialization, commodification and authenticity in heritage tourism, and the relationship between history and heritage.

Similarly, Phillips, Osmond, and Morgan use sport heritage – this time, at a museum – as a means of revealing heritage as both a tool for collective pride and as an instrument for challenging dominant narratives. Many sport heritage narratives, particularly at museums and halls of fame, are about remembering great sporting achievements and, in this, the Ration Shed Museum is no different. However, the role of sporting achievement takes on a much broader social and political context at the Ration Shed Museum, given the history of Aboriginal athletes in Australia. Similarly, sporting achievement in this case also becomes a tool for challenging stereotypes and, as such, these sport heritage narratives provide an even more potent form of inspiration. However, the capacity for heritage to reflect both positive and negative legacies (Lowenthal, 1998; Smith, 2006) is tested here, as the "sport heritage" displayed at the Ration Shed Museum was also about anguish and humiliation. The authors aptly employ James' (2013) *Beyond a Boundary* to this case, revealing that sport – and, perhaps by extension, sport heritage – is a tool for both liberation and subjugation. Perhaps most importantly, these mixed sporting legacies are given a voice, reflecting the wider concern of "whose heritage" is being told and to what end (Hall, 2008). The tourism question is left somewhat ambiguous by the authors, and one has to wonder to what extent sport will be used in the ongoing promotion of the site, and whether tourists seek out the museum based on its association with sport. Similarly, will there be any tension between the cultural and economic ends of this museum (Graham, Ashworth, & Tunbridge, 2000), given that many museums that employ sport, as Vamplew (1998) reminds us, are unabashedly commercial.

Contestation of heritage meanings are also at the heart of Moore, Richardson, and Corkhill's exploration of the annual Tourist Trophy (or TT) motorcycle race on the Isle of Man.

In many ways, the presence of the TT race run quite counter to the rural idyll of the Manx landscape (and, seemingly as well, the island's tourism) though the race itself has become as much a part of the landscape as thatched cottages. However, the heritage contestation comes from largely from memorialization, and how the event and the broader image of the island are perceived. Acknowledgment of sporting feats is already part of the landscape and marked through place names and monuments. In this, the Manx landscape becomes much like the "wall of honour" at a stadium or the "honoured members" section of a sports museum. Naturally, these sections of the landscape are not incongruent with the island's identity and appeal. However, the race is infamous for danger and, at times, death, though this history is not often part of the wider race, or island, heritage. Acknowledgement of negative or dark sport heritages is relatively rare, and often only occurs when there is some benefit in presenting negative narratives (Springwood, 1996). As Moore et al. argue, the TT race is a major part of the Island's tourism and the residents' identity. However, as residents and tourists confront, or are confronted, by alternate interpretations of the race and its casualties, it will be interesting to determine if, and perhaps how, these narratives will be woven into official heritage narratives.

While sport heritage, and the tourism it generates, shares many similarities to other forms of heritage, Gammon reminds us that there are some very distinctive features to sport heritage, namely that much of the fabric of sport heritage – and, indeed, much of what attracts tourists to experience it – are the athletes themselves and the sporting feats they have achieved. Few cultural processes are celebrated like sport and, as Snyder (1991) reminds us, few activities are as widely disseminated, replayed, and relived as sport. The heroes and the sporting moments they create then, as Gammon argues, become artefacts, and though we can relive and replay the achievement (and, in a sense, preserve the moment(s) in time, perhaps through both personal memory and vicariously through media) we cannot preserve "the object" in the same way that we might other forms of tangible heritage. The relationship between the achievement and the athlete, in fact, demonstrates a paradox in sport heritage. Athletes grow old, they change, and they are no longer what they were – indeed, athletes are some of the few heritage "objects" that are not aided by the patina of age. However, their achievements may become more glorious – or heroic – as time goes on. Similarly, if athletes are to be thought of as a "living heritage" (Ramshaw, 2010), then we must understand them as a very dynamic heritage – where their past successes will be determined by present needs, concerns, actions, and opinions. Star athletes still competing today are frequently judged as to their potential "legacy" – that they might help to shape and determine where they and their achievements might fit in the pantheon of a sport's heritage – and that there is an understanding that future behaviour may colour opinions about sport-related legacies. In many respects, and for many athletes, maintaining a legacy – and having a saleable heritage pedigree – is vital for their post-athletics career, and not just for the vast sports memorabilia market but, as Gammon notes, as commodities for the heritage sport tourism market as well.

Finally, the relationship between personal identity, genealogy, and sport heritage is relatively unexplored. The search for roots is at the heart of much of heritage tourism (Timothy, 2011), but how might sport play into these personal journeys, and how might the role of imagination – and the knowingly imprecise nature of heritage – interact with broader cultural interpretations of sport and sport heritage? Ramshaw's autoethnography of his experiences at a county cricket match in England, and how he found it to be quasi-genealogical search for his cricket umpire grandfather, highlights how both personal connections and larger cultural tropes are inevitably intertwined in heritage tourism. Ramshaw found the match to be representative of a quintessential part of English culture, particularly one that is perceived to be under threat, while also finding it to be a longitudinal connection to his family's past. Lowenthal (1998) tells us that blood is the foundational stuff of heritage, so it stands to reason that heritage journeys that involve a search for family roots can be powerful, even if those connections are imaginative in-so-far as they are not a search for objective truth. Ramshaw explains that he knew his grandfather was a cricket umpire in Kent, and that his grandfather had visited the St. Lawrence Ground in Canterbury on several occasions, but that a forensic investigation of his grandfather's cricketing past was not necessary in order to make the experience feel real, meaningful, and powerful. At the same time, however, Ramshaw describes being swept up in the beautiful anachronism of county cricket, where a multiday match reflected something of the heritage of English sport and leisure. Ramshaw's journey necessitates that we must consider heritage sport tourism as something that occurs beyond the boundaries of traditional sport heritage attractions.

Sport can tell us much about heritage and the tourism it inspires. As this collection demonstrates, sport heritage can reflect and illuminate many of the issues, challenges, and debates in heritage and heritage tourism. At other times, sport heritage appears to be a very distinct form of heritage, perhaps because of its broad dissemination and consumption, though perhaps more because of its corporal nature. We have to continue to play sport, or support those who play, in order to create future sport heritage. The fact that sport heritage often does not fossilize, that it must continue to be made and remade through play and performance, is perhaps what gives it a distinctive place in the heritage and heritage tourism landscape.

Acknowledgements

I would like to thank Alana Seaman for her invaluable assistance with this issue.

References

Adair, D. (2004). Where the games never cease: The Olympic Museum in Lausanne, Switzerland. In B. W. Ritchie & D. Adair (Eds.), *Sport tourism: Interrelationships, impacts and issues* (pp. 46–76). Clevedon: Channel View Publications.

Anton, M., Garrett, B. L., Hess, A., Miles, E., & Moreau, T. (2013). London's Olympic waterscape: capturing transition. *International Journal of Heritage Studies, 19*(2), 125–138.

Boukas, N., Ziakas, V., & Boustras, G. (2013). Olympic legacy and cultural tourism: Exploring the facets of Athens' Olympic heritage. *International Journal of Heritage Studies, 19*(2), 203–228.

Brittain, I., Ramshaw, G., & Gammon, S. (2013). The marginalisation of paralympic heritage. *International Journal of Heritage Studies, 19*(2), 171–185.

Cronin, M. (2012). Croke Park: Museum, stadium and shrine for the nation. In M. G. Phillips (Ed.), *Representing the sporting past in museums and halls of fame* (pp. 91–106). London: Routledge.

Day, D., Carter, N., & Carpenter, T. (2013). The Olympics, amateurism and Britain's coaching heritage. *International Journal of Heritage Studies, 19*(2), 139–152.

Friedman, M. (2007). The spectacle of the past: Leveraging history in Fenway Park and Camden Yards. In S. Gammon & G. Ramshaw (Eds.), *Heritage, sport and tourism: Sporting pasts – Tourist futures* (pp. 103–122). London: Routledge.

Gammon, S. (2004). Secular pilgrimage and sport tourism. In B. W. Ritchie & D. Adair (Eds.), *Sport tourism: Interrelationships, impacts and issues* (pp. 30–45). Clevedon: Channel View Publications.

Gammon, S. (2011). "Sporting" new attractions? The commodification of the sleeping stadium. In R. Sharpley & P. Stone (Eds.), *Tourism experiences: Contemporary perspectives* (pp. 115–126). London: Routledge.

Gammon, S., & Fear, V. (2007). Stadia tours and the power of backstage. In S. Gammon & G. Ramshaw (Eds.), *Heritage, sport and tourism: Sporting pasts – tourist futures* (pp. 23–32). London: Routledge.

Graham, B., Ashworth, G. J., & Tunbridge, J. E. (2000). *A geography of heritage: Power, culture & economy*. London: Arnold.

Hall, S. (2008). Whose heritage? Un-settling "The Heritage", re-imagining the post-nation. In G. Fairclough, R. Harrison, J. H. Jameson Jnr., & J. Schofield (Eds.), *The heritage reader* (pp. 219–228). London: Routledge.

Higham, J., & Hinch, T. (2009). *Sport and tourism: Globalization, mobility and identity*. New York: Elsevier.

Hill, J. (2012). Sport, history and imagined pasts. In J. Hill, K. Moore, & J. Wood (Eds.), *Sport, history, and heritage: Studies in public representation* (pp. 9–18). Suffolk: The Boydell Press.

Hinch, T., & de la Barre, S. (2005). Culture, sport and tourism: The case of the Arctic Winter Games. In J. Higham (Ed.), *Sport tourism destinations: Issues, opportunities, and analysis* (pp. 260–273). Oxford: Elsevier Butterworth-Heinemann.

Hinch, T., & Higham, J. (2011). *Sport tourism development* (2nd ed.). Bristol: Channel View Publications.

Hinch, T., & Ramshaw, G. (2014). Heritage sport tourism in Canada. *Tourism Geographies*. Advance online publication. doi:10.1080/14616688.2013.823234

James, C. L. R. (2013). *Beyond a boundary: 50th anniversary edition*. Durham: Duke University Press.

John, G., Sheard, R., & Vickery, B. (2007). *Stadia: A design and development guide* (4th ed.). Oxford: Elsevier.

Joseph, J. (2011). A diaspora approach to sport tourism. *Journal of Sport and Social Issues, 35*(2), 146–167.

Kidd, B. (1996). The making of a hockey artifact: A review of the hockey hall of Fame. *Journal of Sport History, 23*(3), 328–334.

Leask, A., & Digance, J. (2002). Exploiting unused capacity. *Journal of Convention & Exhibition Management, 3*(4), 17–35.

Lowenthal, D. (1998). *The heritage crusade and the spoils of history*. Cambridge: Cambridge University Press.

MacGregor, R. (2006). Forward. In D. Whitson & R. Gruneau (Eds.), *Artificial Ice: Hockey, culture and commerce* (pp. vii–x). Peterborough: Broadview Press.

McGuinness, M. (2012). The canonisation of common people: Memorialization and commemoration in football. In J. Hill, K. Moore, & J. Wood (Eds.), *Sport, history, and heritage: Studies in public representation* (pp. 211–222). Suffolk: The Boydell Press.

O'Neill, M., & Osmond, G. (2012). A racehorse in the Museum: Phar lap and the new museology. In M. G. Phillips (Ed.), *Representing the sporting past in museums and halls of fame* (pp. 29–48). London: Routledge.

Phillips, M. G. (2012). Introduction: Historians in sport museums. In M. G. Phillips (Ed.), *Representing the sporting past in museums and halls of fame* (pp. 1–28). London: Routledge.

Ramshaw, G. (2010). Living heritage and the sports museum: Athletes, legacy and the Olympic hall of fame and museum, Canada Olympic park. *Journal of Sport & Tourism, 15*(1), 45–70.

Ramshaw, G., & Gammon, S. (2005). More than just Nostalgia? Exploring the heritage/sport tourism Nexus. *Journal of Sport Tourism, 10*(4), 229–241.

Ramshaw, G., & Gammon, S. (2010). On home ground? Twickenham stadium tours and the construction of sport heritage. *Journal of Heritage Tourism, 5*(2), 87–102.

Ramshaw, G., Gammon, S., & Huang, W. (2013). Acquired pasts and the commodification of borrowed Heritage: The case of the Bank of America stadium tour. *Journal of Sport & Tourism, 18*(1), 17–31.

Ramshaw, G., & Hinch, T. (2006). Place identity and sport tourism: The case of the heritage classic ice hockey event. *Current Issues in Tourism, 9*(4 & 5), 399–418.

Redmond, G. (1973). A Plethora of Shrines: Sport in the museum and hall of fame. *Quest, 19*, 41–48.

Schultz, J. (2012). Lest we forget: Public history and racial segregation in Baltimore's Druid Hill Park. In M. G. Phillips (Ed.), *Representing the sporting past in museums and halls of fame* (pp. 231–248). London: Routledge.

Smith, J. (2012). Discredited class-war Fable or priceless promotional asset? The duality of Rugby Union's William Webb Ellis foundation myth. In J. Hill, K. Moore, & J. Wood (Eds.), *Sport, history, and heritage: Studies in public representation* (pp. 19–32). Suffolk: The Boydell Press.

Smith, L. (2006). *Uses of heritage*. London: Routledge.

Snyder, E. (1991). Sociology of nostalgia: Sport halls of fame and museums in America. *Sociology of Sport Journal, 8*, 228–238.

Springwood, C. F. (1996). *Cooperstown to Dyersville: A geography of baseball Nostalgia*. Boulder, CO: Westview Press.

Strohmayer, U. (2013). Non-events and their legacies: Parisian heritage and the Olympics that never were. *International Journal of Heritage Studies, 19*(2), 186–202.

Timothy, D. J. (2011). *Cultural heritage and tourism: An introduction*. Bristol: Channel View.

Titterington, A., & Done, S. (2012). Anfield: Relocating Liverpool's spiritual home. In J. Hill, K. Moore, & J. Wood (Eds.), *Sport, history, and heritage: Studies in public representation* (pp. 195–210). Suffolk: The Boydell Press.

Vamplew, W. (1998). Facts and artefacts: Sport historians and sport museums. *Journal of Sport History, 25*(2), 268–282.

Vamplew, W. (2012). Renamed, refurbished and reconstructionist: Comparisons and contrasts in four London sports museums. In M. G. Phillips (Ed.), *Representing the sporting past in museums and halls of fame* (pp. 130–142). London: Routledge.

White, L. (2013). Cathy Freeman and Australia's indigenous heritage: A new beginning for an old nation at the Sydney 2000 Olympic games. *International Journal of Heritage Studies, 19*(2), 153–170.

Williams, J. (2012). The Indianapolis 500: Making the pilgrimage to the "Yard of Bricks". In J. Hill, K. Moore, & J. Wood (Eds.), *Sport, history, and heritage: Studies in public representation* (pp. 247–266). Suffolk: The Boydell Press.

Wright, R. W. (2012). Stadia, identity and belonging: Stirring the sleeping giants of sports tourism. In R. Shipway & A. Fyall (Eds.), *International sports events* (pp. 195–207). London: Routledge.

It still goes on: football and the heritage of the Great War in Britain

Ross J. Wilson

Department of History, University of Chichester, Chichester, West Sussex, UK

This article examines the museum displays and modern memorials that draw on the role of football and footballers in the history of the Great War in Britain. The place of football in the popular memory of the war in Britain is certainly significant at regional and national levels; from the stories of individual footballers and local teams signing up to fight for 'King and Country' to the more famous examples of soldiers kicking a football over no man's land at the Battle of Somme in 1916 and the football game played between opposing combatants during the Christmas Truce of 1914. Museums and memorial sites in Britain and on the former battlefields that reference and represent the place of the sport in the conflict provide places for tourists and pilgrims to remember and mourn these events and the dead. However, the manner in which these sites of memory frame the significance of the game in relationship to the war reveals wider assumptions about the contested memory of the conflict in Britain. Whilst the popular memory of the war focuses on the slaughter of the battlefields and the piteous futility of war, attempts at revising this perception have sought to emphasise the endeavour, commitment and achievement of soldiers. In this battlefield of memory, sports heritage serves as a lens through which issues of contemporary identity in Britain can be established and contested.

Introduction

The First World War still casts a long shadow over British society. Even as the hundredth anniversaries of the conflict draw near, the war still evokes strong responses across communities. To mention the Battle of the Somme, to speak of Passchendaele, Gallipoli or Arras, conjures scenes of devastated landscapes and the abject suffering for the soldiers serving in the 'mud and blood' of the trenches at the behest of their superiors (Wilson, 2009, 2010). However, over the last three decades, this 'popular memory' of the conflict has been challenged by revisionist historians who seek to affirm the significance of Britain's wartime endeavours (Sheffield, 2002). These historians argue that the 'popular memory' has been shaped not by history but by cultural representations of the conflict that emphasise the trauma of the war experience; through novels such as Barker's (1991) *Regeneration*, Faulks's (1993) *Birdsong*, the television series *Blackadder goes forth* (BBC, 1989) or the famous Theatre Workshop (1965) production *Oh! What a lovely war* (Bond, 2002; Todman, 2005). This 'mediated memory' is regarded as obscuring the 'truth' of the war;

that the conflict was fought successfully by Britain's politicians and generals (Gregory, 2008). The popular memory of the piteous suffering of soldiers and the culpability of their leaders is assessed as deriving from modern class-based politics that play upon the sentimentality of the public (Badsey, 2001, 2002). As the hundredth anniversaries draw near, this division poses particular issues for how to present the war and its meanings; as a demonstration of endurance, camaraderie and endeavour or of pity, poignancy and political agendas. These issues are exemplified in the heritage of football and the Great War.

Football and the First World War

After the foundation of the Football Association (1863) and the development of professional clubs (1890s), football dominated male working-class culture by the 1900s (Taylor, 2002, 2008). Therefore, it was perhaps inevitable that it would take a key role with the outbreak of war in 1914. Whilst football had initially attracted criticism for continuing the 1914/ 1915 league season, the game was quickly utilised by the government as both a metaphor for encouraging recruitment and a means of establishing morale within the British Army (Roberts, 2006). With General Kitchener issuing a call to arms in 1914, thousands joined the ranks to serve in the armed forces. After conscription was introduced in 1916, there was a need to ensure the appropriate character within this 'Citizen Army' (Terret, 2011). Indeed, the historian Pollard (1914) wrote in *The Times* in November 1914 of this aspect of football in encouraging health, efficiency and endeavour. As a game known to most volunteers, football was a pastime, but it became increasingly important for the army in instilling the 'fighting spirit' (Mason and Riedi, 2010). Football matches served as a means of developing an attachment to the army and one's comrades. Sir Baden-Powell (1914, p. 150) emphasised this in his military training manual:

> Teach them from the first that they are like bricks in a wall, or players in a football team: each has to be perfect and efficient, each has to adhere patiently to the rules and to play in his place and to play the game.

This concept developed from the public school ethos of the Edwardian era, where the dedication to the team was considered to provide appropriate training for future service to King, Country and Empire (Birley, 1986; Veitch, 1985).

Similarly, the popularity of the sport was used to appeal to the patriotism of working-class men to join the ranks (Simkins, 1988). Football league grounds were offered as potential training sites and match days were accompanied by calls to volunteer. However, working-class professional players were still accused of 'shirking' while 'gentlemen' players fought (Walvin, 1975). Aware of such criticisms, the Football Association encouraged the formation of the 17th Battalion of the Middlesex Regiment as a 'Pals Battalion' in December 1914 (Wyrral, 1926). The 'Pals Battalions' were a recruitment initiative which enabled men of a local area or profession to serve together. The 17th were distinctive, comprisingsome professional footballers and known as the 'Football Battalion' (Riddoch & Kemp, 2008). The recruitment poster for the unit drew upon these associations:

> Do you want to be a Chelsea Diehard? If so, join the 17th Battalion Middlesex Regiment ('the Old Diehards') and follow the lead given by your favourite football players. (IWM PST 0968)

The fate of the Football Battalion was similar to that of many of the Pals Battalions serving on the Western Front in northern France and Flanders; substantial numbers of injuries and fatalities were sustained during the Battle of the Somme (July–November 1916). Similarly, the 'Edinburgh City Pals', the 16th Battalion of the Royal Scots, raised by the prominent Edinburgh businessman Lieutenant Colonel Sir George McCrae, also known as the 'Sporting Battalion', which was drawn from professional players, particularly from Hearts of Midlothian F.C., Raith Rovers F.C. and Hibernian F.C., suffered heavy losses on the Somme (Alexander, 2004). The Reverend Samuel Frederick Leighton Green, serving as an Army Chaplain, described the particular shock of injuries to footballers on the battle-fields, where careers as well as lives could be cut short. The Queens Park Rangers footballer Albert Butler informed the Chaplain of his condition after hospitalisation:

> 'Bad. This leg is done in. No more football for me. I'm a pro...' I look at the papers and see his thigh is shattered...He fights for dear life for ten days, and then goes out. He has played the game. I doubt not he has won. (Leighton Green, 2005, p. 55)

Due to the structure of the Pals Battalions, if heavy losses were sustained in action, then communities, including football clubs, would often find themselves adversely affected by loss. Indeed, during 1916, the 'Sporting Battalion' lost three first team members of Hearts of Midlothian. Over the course of the war, Bradford City F.C. lost nine players, Everton F.C. lost five players, Manchester United lost two players and Newcastle United F.C. suffered the loss of seven players (Harris & Whippy, 2008).

Alongside these tragedies, football was also part of the truce on the Western Front during Christmas Day 1914 when an impromptu game was apparently played (Brown & Seaton, 1984). The truth of the occurrence of the game has been assessed by historians, with some questioning the validity of the claim and others regarding the accounts that emerged in contemporary newspapers and later memoirs as apocryphal (Adams & Petney, 2005). Regardless of the veracity, the notion of soldiers putting down their weapons and playing has become a standard feature of the 'Yuletide Canon', sentimentally referencing the 'triumph of human spirit' (Duffy, 2011). The representations of the Christmas Day football match, whilst forming part of a 'national narrative' within Britain, also conceives of a wider international community and a means to move beyond the commemoration of the nation state (Foreman, 2006). Conversely, the other football event during the war which has been used to emphasise the 'British' character is the 'football charge' led by Captain W.P Nevill of the East Surrey Regiment during the Battle of the Somme (Adams, 2012). Captain Nevill brought footballs to the front to reassure and encourage his men, possibly inspired by an earlier incident, where members of the London Irish Rifles kicked a football during advances at the Battle of Loos (1915) (Harris, 2009). Though Nevill was killed in the offensive, his actions were widely reported at the time as indicative of the 'British spirit' (Fussell, 1975, pp. 28–29).

History, heritage and memory

The fusion of sport and nationalism in Captain Nevill's charge is indicative of the wider manner in which football is perceived within Britain. As the 'national game', scholarly assessments of football history and heritage have examined its prominent place and value within British society throughout the twentieth century (Walvin, 1975). Commentators have all drawn attention to the way in which the game has provided a common cultural reference point in Britain (Armstrong & Giulianotti, 1997; Harvey, 2005; Wagg, 2004). Recent examinations of sports heritage and tourism studies, including stadia visits, historic football grounds, museums and memorials have also drawn attention to this capacity of the game (Gammon & Fear, 2005, 2007). Whether national, corporate or community in character, football heritage sites frequently rely upon the 'communal experience' of watching or participating (Hood, 2006). This is certainly evident with the opening of the Scottish National Football Museum in 2001 at Hampden Park, Glasgow, and the National Football Museum which opened first in 2004 in Preston before relocating to Manchester in 2012 (Moore, 2012). Both institutions present the history of the game as evident of a 'national characteristic':

> The National Football Museum exists to explain how and why football has become 'the people's game', a key part of England's heritage and way of life. It also aims to explain why England is the home of football, the birthplace of the world's most popular sport. (National Football Museum, 2012)

> The Scottish Football Museum exists to promote the unique football heritage of Scotland, to build and maintain a national football collection, and to educate and inspire future generations. (Scottish Football Museum, 2012)

A critical appraisal of the role of football and the construction of identity through tourist sites has been neglected as studies have focused on the economic capacity of this aspect of sports heritage (Moore, 2008). However, the relationship between football and the First World War provides an opportunity to assess how football heritage tourism constructs and maintains identity (McGuinness, 2012).

Scholars have assessed how sports heritage contributes significantly to the role of identity formation, both local and national, through the imposition of meanings and associations onto places and objects (Gammon, 2007; Gammon & Ramshaw, 2007; Hill, Moore, & Wood, 2012; Ramshaw, 2006; Ramshaw & Gammon, 2005, 2007). This work has taken a critical perspective, assessing 'sports heritage' as a process through which social and political norms are replicated (Harvey, 2001). As Smith (2006) has stated, the construction of 'heritage' is an acceptance of the values attached to the term which authorises a hegemonic socio-political discourse that marginalises political, social, economic, ethnic and gender issues that are present within society. However, this obscured heritage can also be used to disrupt these dominant narratives and to provide subaltern histories to challenge established norms (Smith, 2006, p. 35). Sports heritage studies have utilised this affirming and dissonant definition of heritage as a means to critique issues of race, equality and gender representation (Ramshaw & Gammon, 2005). In this manner, analyses of sports tourism have demonstrated how institutional representations of sporting pasts are constructed and problematised through often conflicting aspects of 'heritage' (Gammon, Ramshaw, & Waterton, 2012; Phillips, 2012).

This concept of heritage is highly pertinent in consideration of the popular memory and revisionist interpretations of the Great War. The historic sites, museums and memorials which provide visitors with a means to engage with the history and heritage of football and the conflict of 1914–1918 can be assessed on the basis of their representations (Moore, 2008). These depictions serve as mediums through which competing visions/discourses of the war are accessed and consumed by visitors. They are, therefore, central in the construction and maintenance of memory with regard to the First World War in Britain. These sites also offer a means to comment on the disparity between the 'popular' and 'revisionist' interpretations of the First World War. As the history of football and the First World War evokes the poignancy and the 'pity of war' alongside the narratives of achievement and endeavour, the ability of tourist sites to represent this 'battlefield of memory' will be of especial importance within the context of the centenary of the conflict. The case studies presented below, which detail the sports heritage of the First World War, highlight how tourist sites are used to construct narratives and identities which shape the understanding of the war and its relevance for contemporary society.

The footballs and footballers of the battlefields

A number of institutions across Britain include footballs associated with the conflict of 1914–1918. The most notable are those used in advances across no man's land by the London Irish at the Battle of Loos (1915) and those kicked by Captain W.P. Nevill at the Battle of the Somme (1916). The Surrey Infantry Museum (2012) at Clandon Park houses one of the footballs retrieved from the battlefields that were used by Nevill and his men. Although housed in a wider collection of artefacts from the conflict and from other theatres of war in which Surrey soldiers served, Nevill's football takes a prominent place in the museum's display. Located in the exhibition case for the First World War, the football is surrounded by the military accoutrements of the British Army. Located beside weapons, a mannequin in full uniform, and within a reconstructed trench setting, the football is given a martial quality befitting of the use of the game by Nevill. The representation of the war, through this piece of football heritage, is one of achievement. Indeed, the object is framed within the bellicose news reporting of the era, accompanied as it is by a newspaper article of July 1916 which greeted the return of the football to the battalion where it is described as a 'sacred emblem of the battalion's heroism and devotion'. This presentation of the football within a military museum is replicated in the exhibition of the other football used by Captain Nevill in the Princess of Wales's Royal Regiment Museum (2013) at Dover Castle. Within this display, the football is once again located within the context of heroic endeavour, with a Lee Enfield Rifle, the standard weapon issued to British soldiers, leaning next to the football. Once again, the display is within a reconstructed trench setting, with uniformed mannequins manning machine guns and lining up ready to go 'over the top'. The accompanying display panel reiterates the gallantry of the action:

> His football was inscribed 'The Great European Cup Final – East Surreys vs Bavarians'. Another was marked 'No Referee'.

The reference to the absence of officials refers to the encouragement of troops to give their enemies no quarter on the field of battle but has also been interpreted by authors as evidence of the characteristic, laconic humour of the British (Fussell, 1975). Similarly, the London Irish Rifles Association Museum (2012), which houses the football kicked across the battlefield of Loos, is also placed within the context of endeavour and achievement alongside the artefacts of the London Irish's service in wartime. Through this arrangement, visitor experiences are structured through a particular vision of the conflict of 1914–1918 as a suitably noble sacrifice. This is also reflected in the displays of the achievements of wartime footballers in the football museums across Britain. In the National Football Museum in Manchester, the displays regarding the conflict of 1914–1918 demonstrate the mobilisation of football and footballers for the war effort (Figure 1). The panels enable the visitor to learn of Donald Simpson Bell (1890–1916), who played for Crystal Palace F.C. and Newcastle United and who was the only footballer to win the Victoria Cross medal for his bravery on the field of conflict. The medal is displayed alongside the bullet-damaged helmet worn by Bell who died a week after his commendation on 10 July 1916 in the early period of fighting during the Battle of the Somme. The connection between service

Figure 1. Donald Simpson Bell Display, National Football Museum, Manchester (Photo by author. Courtesy of the National Football Museum).

and sacrifice is therefore reiterated as visitors bear witness to the achievements of the footballers who served their country. This perspective is also furthered through the display of wartime football. Recruitment posters encouraging footballers across the country to sign up are part of the exhibition which emphasises the martial connections between fighting war and playing football. One poster from the Central London Recruiting Depot in 1914 featured in the exhibition states:

Young men of Britain! The Germans said you were not in earnest. 'We knew you'd come – and give them the lie!" Play the greater game and join the football battalion.

A display of a child's game of 'Trench Football' also demonstrates this close association between football and the war. 'Trench Football' requires the player to 'dribble' a ball through a maze of trenches before 'scoring' in the German lines through the mouth of a comical depiction of the head of the Germany Imperial Army, Kaiser Wilhelm II. The 'normalisation' of the war through the common social element of football is an implicit aspect of this display which provides the visitor with a demonstration of the game's service to the nation and its players' sacrifices for 'King and Country' (Mosse, 1990, pp. 140–141).

War memorials and monuments to footballers

Where a distinct challenge to this discourse of football and national endeavour is located is within the construction of sites of commemoration. Tourists visiting these sites are able to access the history of the war not as a national sacrifice, emphasising the links between the war and the 'people's game', but as an exercise in evoking the poignancy and the pity of war. Visitors to these commemorative sites are not presented with the place of football in the service of the war but with the emotional side of young lives lost and futures left unfulfilled. Studies of contemporary tourism and the commemorative landscape on the former battlefields and the memorialisation of the war dead through monuments across the cities, towns and villages of Britain have highlighted the manner in which experiences are structured through this material presence (Iles, 2008, 2011; Winter, 2012). In the immediate aftermath of the war, a symbolic commemoration of the war dead was enabled through memorials and monuments which stressed the nature of sacrifice and martial endeavour for Britain and Empire (Bushaway, 1992; Heffernan, 1995). In this schema, individual death was subsumed into a wider national and imperial narrative, where distinctions of rank, occupation and position are ameliorated to promote the idea of collective endeavour (Lacquer, 1994). However, over the last two decades, a shift in the habits and forms of the cultural memory of the First World War has shifted attention towards individual and local recognition (Moriarty, 1999, 2007). This has been accompanied by a new wave of commemoration, as memorials in various locations are constructed to remember the 'specific dead' of a region, group or occupation, as opposed to the collective, national 'glorious dead' commemorated through postwar memorials such as the Cenotaph in Whitehall, London.

This alteration in memory is demonstrated most clearly in the development of memorials to mark the lives and deaths of footballers during the war. Individual and groups of footballers have been commemorated throughout Britain and these aspects of sports heritage present an intriguing, though neglected, source of study (Russell, 2006). Through these memorials, what is recalled for the visitor is not the service of the footballer to the nation, but the pity of life lost and the sentimentality of the destruction of an individual's physical presence for one who relied upon their physicality to earn their living (Bourke, 1996). One of the first footballers to be commemorated in this manner was Second Lieutenant Walter Tull (1888–1918). Tull's legacy as one of the first black officers in the British Army and one of the first black players at the highest level has entailed that he constitutes a very particular part of the sports heritage of the conflict (Vasili, 2009). Though largely forgotten in the post-war era, from the 1990s onwards, Tull has been reclaimed as an important part of African British history as well as Britain's football heritage (Vasili, 1996). Studies of Tull's life, his career as a footballer and as a soldier in the Footballers Battalion, encouraged a campaign for a memorial to be erected in his honour. The memorial, which was dedicated in 1999, was placed adjacent to the Sixfields Stadium which since 1994 has been the home ground of Northampton Town, Tull's last football club before he joined the Footballers Battalion in 1914. The memorial lists both Tull's army and football career, but its epitaph draws attention to another capacity of this commemoration:

> Through his actions, Tull ridiculed the barriers of ignorance that tried to deny people of colour equality with their contemporaries. His life stands testament to a determination to confront those people and those obstacles that sought to diminish him and the world in which he lived. It reveals a man, though rendered breathless in his prime, whose strong heart still beats loudly.

The heritage of this sporting figure is thereby used to transcend the standard association between football, the army and the nation by demonstrating the complexity of individual experience and concepts of identity. Indeed, Tull has been presented within political and educational initiatives as a means of emphasising the long-standing African Caribbean presence in Britain:

> It reminds everyone...that black Britons have been contributing to our society for many years. (Black History for Schools, 2001)

> As the first black infantryman in the British Army, and my home team's first black player, I'm proud of Walter Tull's contribution to his country. (David Lammy (MP) as cited in Northamptonshire Black History Association, 2007, p. 5)

In effect, the memorialisation of Walter Tull, the footballer and the soldier, is used to evidence the heterogeneous nature of British society both during Tull's lifetime and within contemporary Britain (Vasili, 2009). The memorial also provides a means for Northampton Town's new stadium to draw association to the club's past. The club's Armistice Day memorial services are held next to the memorial site and wreaths for the dead are laid at the base of Tull's memorial. Indeed, the road behind the memorial adjacent to the stadium has been renamed 'Walter Tull Way' to evoke the same appearance of history. However, what is significant about this 'recovered' heritage is the manner in which Tull's experiences are framed. This is a history and heritage for visitors which is presented as a sporting and political legacy, beyond the intimate associations of football and military service that are expressed within the regimental and national football museums. The sports heritage of the war of 1914–1918 is thereby used to revise and challenge dominant ideas about identity within Britain (Gammon, 2007). This representation which focuses upon how Tull's life was cut short on the Western Front relies upon an emotional appeal of the suffering soldier on the battlefields which visitors to the site can place within the wider popular memory of the First World War in Britain.

This use of memorials is also evident in the recent construction of sites of remembrance to those footballers who died during the conflict. For example, Everton F.C. revealed a black marble plaque outside their Goodison Park stadium in 2011 listing the names of seven former footballers who died in the war. The plaque is placed purposefully next to a statue of the 'club legend' Dixie Dean (1907–1980), as tours of the ground commemorate the pity of war and the loss of sporting life rather than national military endeavour (Griffiths, 2011). Dr David France, the philanthropist and businessman who funded the project, promoted this image of the soldier at the unveiling of the plaque:

> So I was interested in that, and these days you can research things really well. Just think of it, some say Jack Rodwell (former Everton player) at 20 is not old enough to play in the first team

yet, not experienced enough – these lads were in the trenches risking and losing their lives (as cited in O'Keefe, 2011, p. 25)

A similar remembrance scheme can be noted in the earlier memorial to the footballers from Aberdeen F.C. which was placed in their Pittodrie Stadium in 2009. The memorial consists of a framed Aberdeen shirt, embroidered with a memorial poppy, with details of the Aberdeen footballers who served accompanied by the invocation 'Lest We Forget'. The memorial now features in stadium tours commemorated eight members of the pre-war Aberdeen team who died in the conflict and poppy wreaths are now placed at the site on every Armistice Day (Aberdeen F.C. Heritage Trust, 2009). These individual memorials for players and clubs serve to evoke the pity of war, echoing the popular memory of the conflict, focused as they are on reminding visitors of the loss of life and the tragedy of death.

In foreign fields: football memorials on the Western Front

It is not only within Britain that memorials to the dead footballers of the war can be located. Indeed, the sports heritage of the First World War can be located in a number of recent memorials across France and Belgium. These tourist sites provide visitors with an alternative means of commemoration, striking a contrast with the vast collective forms of remembrance through the cemeteries and memorials that were constructed in the post-1918 era. These memorials are recent additions to the commemorative landscape, demonstrating the changing forms and habits of memory but also emphasising the different tourist experiences that are evoked through the remembrance of 'fallen footballers' not 'fallen soldiers'. For example, in 2004, a memorial to the 16th Royal Scots was unveiled on the site of the French village of Contalmaison which was on the front line of the Battle of the Somme in 1916 where many from the battalion were killed. The memorial to the 16th (the 'Sporting Battalion') was entirely funded by public donation and closely allied with Hearts of Midlothian Football Club who assisted in developing the scheme. Edinburgh City Council (2004, p. 3) also supported the project as a means of commemorating the loss of life during the conflict:

> It seems entirely appropriate that in 2004, the centenary of the signing of the Entente Cordiale with France, proper recognition should be given to those Edinburgh men who sacrificed their lives. The association with Heart of Midlothian Football Club has ensured that their memory lives on in the city and the proposed memorial cairn in Contalmaison will replicate this in France, where they fell.

The memorial consists of a large cairn, made from Scottish sandstone, upon which four memorial plaques made by a Scottish blacksmith have been placed, commemorating those who fought in the battle. One plaque depicts both soldiers and footballers, whilst also bearing the emblem of Hearts of Midlothian replete with the sentimental verse:

> Come pack up your footballs and scarves of maroon,
> Leave all your sweethearts in Auld Reekie toon,
> Fall in wi' the lads for they're off and away,
> To take on the bold Hun with old Geordie McCrae,
> Rest in Peace Boys

The memorial cairn now plays an important part in battlefield tours, serving as a point of remembrance for visitors to the site (Waterloo Tours, 2012). Hearts supporters and those with connections to the 'Sporting Battalion' congregate every year at the memorial to mark the anniversary of the Battle of the Somme. The tourist site, therefore, inculcates a number of effects through its evocation of the footballer soldiers of the 16th Royal Scots. First, tourists are reminded of a particular Scottish as opposed to 'British' or 'English' identity, constructed through the materiality of the cairn as well as demonstrated in the campaign for its erection. The memorial serves to remember Scottish sporting heroes and their deaths in battle:

> It is vital that this and future generations of Scots know about this critical period of our history and what these brave men did. That is what Remembrance Day is all about. (Scottish Government, 2004)

Second, visitors are provided with an image of the tragedy of war, demonstrated in the reference on the monument's plaque to 'sweethearts' and to 'fall in wi' the lads'. In this fashion, notions of identity are constructed through this sporting heritage of the piteous nature of conflict. The juxtaposition of this personal consideration of loss with the official post-war commemorative memorials which focus on collective 'national' sacrifice reflects the capacity of sports heritage to disrupt official narratives.

This reliance on the emotive appeal of the conflict and the tragic status of the war within British 'popular memory' can be evidenced with the construction of a memorial to all members of the Footballers' Battalion near the Somme village of Longueval. The memorial was funded by donations from the members of the football league in England and Wales and unveiled in October 2010 (Football League, 2010). The memorial, comprising a black granite headstone topped with a sculptured, stitched football, was unveiled by members of the Football League, the Professional Footballers Association and the Football Supporters Federation. The memorial's subject of 'fallen footballers' and its location on the site of the battlefields which witnessed the largest number of fatalities in British military history connect the remembrance of the footballer's battalion to the commemoration of the 'pity of war'. At the foot of the memorial is inscribed a wartime quote from a serving member of the battalion: 'This is worse than a whole season of cup ties'. However, the memorial also reminds visitors of the sacrifice of soldiers for the nation. Sporting heritage is in this regard mobilised once again to recall the concepts of the 'greater game' expressed within wartime recruitment campaigns. The main inscription of the memorial illustrates this connection as it marks those who 'served their game and their country during the Great War'. The memorial site, therefore, not only serves as a means for tourists to recall the tragedy of lives lost but to place the game of football 'into perspective', to emphasise the identity of these men as soldiers aiding their country in the time of war (Football League, 2010).

This reliance on the authorised narrative of sporting heritage can be contrasted with the other major episode of the war that involved football: the game supposedly played during the Christmas Truce of 1914. The moment when opposing British and German soldiers laid down their weapons and organised a ceasefire has often been regarded as an example of humanity in the midst of carnage. However, marking the event has been, in the main, the preserve of authors and artists, largely due to the contested nature of the Christmas Truce as historians have challenged some of the accounts from the period (Brown & Seaton, 1984). Nevertheless, in recent years there have emerged points in the memorial landscape where visitors can remember the events of Christmas 1914 and the moment when opposing soldiers became just opposing football players. A memorial for the truce was erected in the village of Frelinghien, northern France in November 2008, commemorating the truce between the 2nd Royal Welch Fusiliers and the Jäger-Battalion of the Germany Army. To mark the unveiling, a football match was played between current members of the British and German militaries. The memorial now serves as a tourist site for visitors to recall the Christmas Truce and the moment when football became a means of bridging national divides.

This agenda can also be located in moves to historicise the football match played during the Christmas Truce of 1914. Indeed, in 2009 plans emerged to build a football ground by 2014 near the battlefields in Flanders to honour the Christmas Truce as an example for current generations (Mullan, 2011). Named the 'Flanders Peace Field', the site is designed to promote reconciliation across the world using the image of the impromptu game conducted on Christmas Day 1914. For example, during the centenary, children's friendly games between former combatant nations have been organised (National Children's Football Alliance, 2013). De Keersmaeker (2012), President of the Belgian Football Association, reflected upon this potential of this sports heritage to challenge ideas:

> A particular lesson we get from the Christmas Truces is that Football is NOT war, despite of what some people say! On the contrary, football connects people, football overcomes differences, football strengthens people and football can be an amplifier on the path to a better world.

The ground would, therefore, serve as a 'living' piece of sports heritage, acting as a site of re-enactment for visitors as they participate in and observe football games. The transition from perceiving the soldier to recognising the soccer player is enabled by this process as the heritage of the war is regarded beyond national boundaries. A sentimental regard for the football match of December 1914 is mobilised to effect alternative identities with regard to the war. Significantly, the organisers of the site envisioned the understanding of the past beyond national boundaries and military associations, requiring visitors to remove themselves from 'entrenched' positions:

> Visit Flanders Peace Field; bring your family and friends. Play football and games. Encounter other people from around the world and realise that strangers are friends waiting to be discovered. The world needs peacemakers. It needs us all to step out of our trenches and cross the No Man's Land of ignorance, prejudice and violence. (Mullan, 2011, p. 114)

As a tourist site, the 'Flanders Peace Field' would occupy another locale on the 'heritage trail' along the battlefields which have become a significant focus for the Government of Flanders which has increasingly marketed the commemorative landscape as an 'international' and 'intercultural' site (Government of Flanders, 2011). The 'In Flanders Field Museum' (2012) in Ieper exemplifies this approach with a dedicated multinational agenda that promotes the places of conflict as international sites of mourning. The museum exhibition also features an art installation depicting the Christmas Truce to emphasise the moment of humanity in an industrialised conflict. In the context of the centenary, this will undoubtedly broaden the appeal for European and international visitors, but the Government of Flanders's '2014–2018' focus on 'war and peace', 'remembrance and awareness' and 'the European idea' also ensures a transcendence of national objectives towards a sentimental idealism (Government of Flanders, 2013). Therefore, commemorations of the 'Christmas Truce' provide a means for tourists to the region to reflect not on national endeavour but the ways in which the game, and sport more generally, provides a means of addressing shared issues. Those who emerged from the trenches on Christmas 1914, regardless of whether a ball was produced and a game of football was played, are thereby represented to visitors not as opposing soldiers but as individuals with common interests. Therefore, this aspect of the sports heritage of football during the Great War operates to challenge the established means of national identification through the commemoration of the war by attempting an international perspective.

Conclusions: the intangible heritage of the conflict

The heritage of football and the Great War provides an intriguing means to assess the function of the memory of the conflict within contemporary British society. Football formed a significant means to mobilise the population in Britain for the war, operating as both a metaphor and a motivator for serving 'King and Country'. The presentation of this past within football museums and memorial sites can act to perpetuate the association between the game and the war. In this manner, these sites of memory offer a perspective that reiterates the revisionist memory of the war in Britain as a noble endeavour; football becomes an illustrative device to frame the concept of service. However, this assessment of the football heritage of the conflict is challenged by various regional and international memorial sites that stress the identity of individuals as footballers not just as soldiers. The shift in this representation is significant; enabling the visitor to access the past through the medium of sport rather than a militarist, national framework. Revealing a history which is composed of players not soldiers provides a means for visitors to utilise aspects of the popular memory of the war in Britain. It is this popular memory which is characterised by a sentimental, sympathetic engagement that transcends concepts of national service and sacrifice and mobilises issues of humanity, pacifism and peace. Rather than merely serving as an interesting addendum to the history of the conflict, the sports heritage of the Great War demonstrates its capacity to impact on the vision of both the past and the present.

References

Aberdeen Heritage Trust. (2009). *World War One memorial event*. Retrieved from http://www. afcheritage.org/news/news_story.cfm?news_id=7200&newstype=Heritage

Adams, I. (2012). Over the top: 'A Foul; a Blurry Foul!' *The International Journal of the History of Sport, 29*(6), 813–831.

Adams, I., & Petney, T. (2005). Germany 3 – Scotland 2, no man's land, 25th December, 1914: Fact or fiction? In J. Magee, A. Bairner, & Alan Tomlinson (Eds.), *The bountiful game? Football identities and finances* (pp. 21–41). Oxford: Meyer & Meyer.

Alexander, J. (2004). *McCrae's Battalion: The story of the 16th Royal Scots*. Edinburgh: Mainstream Publishing.

Armstrong, G., & Giulianotti, R. (Eds.). (1997). *Entering the field: New perspectives on world football*. Oxford: Berg.

Baden-Powell, R. (1914). *Quick training for war*. London: Herbert Jenkins.

Badsey, S. (2001). Blackadder goes forth and the 'two Western Fronts' debate. In G. Roberts and P.M. Taylor (Eds.), *The historian, television and television history* (pp. 113–125). Luton: University of Luton Press.

Badsey, S. (2002). The Great War since the Great War. *Historical Journal of Film, Radio and Television, 22*(1), 7–19.

Barker, P. (1991). *Regeneration*. London: Penguin.

BBC. (1989). *Blackadder goes forth* (dir. R. Boden).

Birley, D. (1986). Sportsmen and the deadly game. *British Journal of Sports History, 3*, 288–310.

Black History for Schools. (2001). *Black footballers*. Retrieved from http://www.blackhistory4schools. com/20century/blackfootballers.pdf

Bond, B. (2002). *The unquiet Western Front*. Cambridge: Cambridge University Press.

Bourke, J. (1996). *Dismembering the British male: Men's bodies, Britain and the Great War*. London: Routledge.

Brown, M., & Seaton, S. (1984). *Christmas Truce: The Western Front, December 1914*. London: Imperial War Museum.

Bushaway, B. (1992). Name upon name: The Great War and remembrance. In R. Porter (Ed.), *Myths of the English* (pp. 136–167). Cambridge: Polity.

De Keersmaeker, F. (2012). *Flanders peace fields press conference 25/1/12*. Retrieved from http://www.mechelsehattrick.be/uploads/1/7/5/1/1751232/fpf_-_speech_francois_de_keersmaecker.pdf

Duffy, C. A. (2011). *The Christmas Truce*. London: Picador.

Edinburgh City Council. (2004). *Hearts Great War memorial fund – memorial at Contalmaison, France*. Retrieved from http://www.edinburgh.gov.uk/download/meetings/id/4646/hearts_great_war_memorial_fund-memorial_at_contalmaison_france

Faulks, S. (1993). *Birdsong*. London: Vintage.

Football League. (2010). *Memorial for the 17th and 23rd Middlesex 'The footballers' battalions', 11:00am, 21st October 2010, Longueval, The Somme, France*. London: Image Directors.

Foreman, M. (2006). *War game: Village green to no-man's-land*. London: Anova Books.

Fussell, P. (1975). *The Great War and modern memory*. Oxford: Oxford University Press.

Gammon, S. (2007). Introduction: Sport, heritage and the English. An opportunity missed? In S. Gammon & G. Ramshaw (Eds.), *Heritage, sport and tourism: Sporting pasts – tourist futures* (pp. 1–8). London: Routledge.

Gammon, S., & Fear, V. (2005). Stadia tours and the power of backstage. *The Journal of Sport Tourism, 10*(4), 243–252.

Gammon, S., & Fear, V. (2007). Stadia tours and the power of backstage. In S. Gammon & G. Ramshaw (Eds.), *Heritage, sport and tourism: Sporting pasts – tourist futures* (pp. 23–33). London: Routledge.

Gammon, S., & Ramshaw, G. (Eds.). (2007). *Heritage, sport and tourism: Sporting pasts – tourist futures*. London: Routledge.

Gammon, S., Ramshaw, G., & Waterton, E. (2012). Examining the Olympics: Heritage, identity and performance. *International Journal of Heritage Studies, 19*(2), 119–124.

Government of Flanders. (2011). *The Great War centenary (2014–18)*. Brussels: Government of Flanders.

Government of Flanders. (2013). *The Great War centenary (2014-'18)*. Retrieved from http://www.vlaanderen.be/int/en/great-war-centenary-2014-18

Gregory, A. (2008). *The last Great War: British society and the First World War*. Cambridge: Cambridge University Press.

Griffiths, D. (2011). *Goodison war memorial unveiled*. Retrived from http://www.evertonfc.com/news/archive/2011/06/29/goodison-war-memorial-unveiled

Harris, C., & Whippy, J. (2008). *The greater game: Sporting icons who fell in the Great War*. London: Pen and Sword.

Harris, Ed. (2009). *The footballer of Loos: A story of the 1st battalion London Irish rifles in the First World War*. Sutton: Stroud.

Harvey, A. (2005). *Football: The first hundred years*. London: Routledge.

Harvey, D. C. (2001). Heritage pasts and heritage presents: Temporality, meaning and the scope of heritage studies. *International Journal of Heritage Studies, 7*(4), 319–338.

Heffernan, M. (1995). For ever England: The Western Front and the politics of remembrance in Britain. *Ecumene, 2*(3), 293–323.

Hill, J., Moore, K., & Wood, J. (Eds.). (2012). *Sport, history, and heritage: Studies in public representation*. London: Boydell and Brewer.

Hood, A. (2006). *Sport heritage network mapping survey: An overview of sports heritage collections. Commissioned by the sports heritage network*. London: Museums, Libraries and Archives Council.

Iles, J. (2008). Encounters in the fields – Tourism to the battlefields of the Western Front. *Journal of Tourism and Cultural Change, 6*(2), 138–154.

Iles, J. (2011). Going on holiday to imagine war: The Western Front battlefields as sites of commemoration and contestation. In D. Theodossopoulos & J. Skinner (Eds.), *Great expectations: Imagination and anticipation in tourism* (pp. 155–173). Oxford: Berg.

IWM PST 0968. Do you want to be a Chelsea die-hard. Imperial War Museum, London.

Lacquer, T. (1994). Memory and naming in the Great War. In J. Gillis (Ed.), *Memory and commemoration* (pp. 150–168). Princeton: Princeton University Press.

Leighton Green, S. (2005). *Somewhere in Flanders: A Norfolk Padre in the Great War. The War letters of the Revd Samuel Frederick Leighton Green MC, Army Chaplain, 1916–1919*. Norwich: The Larks Press.

London Irish Rifles Association Museum. (2012). *Regimental museum*. Retrieved from http://www.londonirishrifles.com/museum

Mason, T., & Riedi, E. (2010). *Sport and the military: The British armed forces 1880–1960*. Cambridge: Cambridge University Press.

McGuinness, M. (2012). The canonisation of common people: Memorialisation and commemoration in football. In J. Hill, K. Moore, & J. Wood (Eds.), *Sport, history, and heritage: Studies in public representation* (pp. 211–222). Woodbridge: Boydell.

Moore, K. (2008). Sports heritage and the re-imaged city: The national football museum, Preston. *International Journal of Cultural Policy, 14*(4), 445–461.

Moore, K. (2012). Sport in museums and museums of sport: An overview. In J. Hill, K. Moore & J. Wood (Eds.), *Sport, history, and heritage: Studies in public representation* (pp. 93–106). Woodbridge: Boydell.

Moriarty, C. (1999). The material culture of Great War remembrance. *Journal of Contemporary History, 34*(4), 653–662.

Moriarty, C. (2007). Private grief and public remembrance. In M. Evans & K. Lunn (Eds.), *War and memory in the twentieth century* (pp. 125–142). Oxford: Berg.

Mosse, G. (1990). *Fallen soldiers: Reshaping the memory of the World Wars*. Oxford: Oxford University Press.

Mullan, D. (2011). Christmas Truce project. In J. O'Halloran (Ed.), *Building community: Vision and practice* (pp. 105–114). Blackrock: Columba.

National Children's Football Alliance. (2013). *The Christmas truce & Flanders peace field project*. Retrieved from http://www.childrensfootballalliance.com/the-christmas-truce-flanders-peace-field-project/

National Football Museum. (2012). *Mission and vision*. Retrieved from http://www.nationalfootball museum.com/about-us/mission-and-vision/

Northamptonshire Black History Association. (2007). Walter Tull. *Northamptonshire Black History Association Newsletter, 5*(4), 5.

O'Keefe, G. (2011, June 29). BLUES HONOUR FALLEN HEROES: New plaque memorial for war dead. *Liverpool Echo*, p. 25.

Phillips, M. (2012). Introduction – Historians in sport museums. In M. Phillips (Ed.), *Representing the sporting past in museums and halls of fame* (pp. 1–26). New York: Routledge.

Pollard, A. F. (1914, November 7). Letter. *The Times*.

Princess of Wales's Royal Regiment Museum. (2013). *Royal regiment museum*. Retrieved from http://www.dover-castle-friends.org/tour/royal_regiment_museum/

Ramshaw, G. (2006). Heritage sport tourism: Development and perspectives. In P. Bouchet & C. Pigeassou, (Eds.), *Sport management: Issues and perspectives* (pp. 409–420). Montpellier: Association Francophone Recherche Activité Physique Sportive.

Ramshaw, G., & Gammon, S. (2005). More than just nostalgia? Exploring the heritage/sport tourism nexus. *The Journal of Sport Tourism, 10*(4), 229–241.

Ramshaw, G., & Gammon, S. (2007). More than just nostalgia? Exploring the heritage/sport tourism nexus. In S. Gammon & G. Ramshaw (Eds.), *Heritage, sport and tourism: Sporting pasts – tourist futures* (pp. 9–22). London: Routledge.

Riddoch, A., & Kemp, J. (2008). *When the whistle blows: The story of the footballers' battalion in the Great War*. Bristol: Haynes.

Roberts, J. (2006). 'The best football team, the best platoon': The role of football in the proletarianization of the British expeditionary force, 1914–1918. *Sport in History, 26*(1), 26–46.

Russell, D. (2006). We all agree, name the stand after Shankly: Cultures of commemoration in late twentieth-century English football culture. *Sport in History, 26*(1), 1–25.

Scottish Football Museum. (2012). *About the museum*. Retrieved from http://www.scottishfootball museum.org.uk/the-museum/about.html

Scottish Government. (2004). *French memorial to Scottish soldiers*. Retrieved from http://www.scotland.gov.uk/News/Releases/2004/11/03154039

Sheffield, G. (2002). *Forgotten victory, the First World War – Myths and realities*. London: Review.

Simkins, P. (1988). *Kitchener's army: The raising of the new armies, 1914–16*. Manchester: Manchester University Press.

Smith, L. (2006). *Uses of heritage*. London: Routledge.

Surrey Infantry Museum. (2012). *Surrey infantry museum at Clandon Park*. Retrieved from http://www.queensroyalsurreys.org.uk/new_museum/new_museum.shtml

Taylor, M. (2002). Work and play: The professional footballer in England c.1900–1950. *The Sports Historian, 22*(1), 16–43.

Taylor, M. (2008). *The association game: A history of British football*. Edinburgh: Pearson.

Terret, T. (2011). Prologue: Making men, destroying bodies: Sport, masculinity and the Great War experience. *The International Journal of the History of Sport, 28*(4), 323–328.

Theatre Workshop. (1965). *Oh! What a lovely war*. London: Methuen.

Todman, D. (2005). *The Great War: Myth and memory*. London: Hambledon.

Vasili, P. (1996). Walter Daniel Tull, 1888–1918: Soldier, footballer, black. *Race and Class, 38*(2), 51–69.

Vasili, P. (2009). *Walter Tull, 1888–1918: Officer, footballer: 'All the guns in France couldn't wake me'*. London: Raw Press.

Veitch, C. (1985). Play up! play up! and win the war! Football, the nation and the First World War. *Journal of Contemporary History, 20*, 363–377.

Wagg, S. (Ed.). (2004). *British football and social exclusion*. London: Routledge.

Walvin, J. (1975). *The people's game: A social history of British football*. London: Allen Lane.

Waterloo Tours. (2012). *Footballers of the Great War*. Retrieved from http://www.waterlootours.co.uk/uploads/Footballers%20Tour%2018–20%20May%202012%20Itinerary.pdf

Wilson, R. (2009). Memory and trauma: Narrating the Western Front, 1914–1918. *Rethinking History, 13*(2), 251–268.

Wilson, R. (2010). The popular memory of the Western Front: Archaeology and European heritage. In E. Waterton & S. Watson (Eds.), *Cultural heritage and representation: Perspectives on visuality and the past* (pp. 75–90). Aldershot: Ashgate.

Winter, C. (2012). Commemoration of the Great War on the Somme: Exploring personal connections. *Journal of Tourism and Cultural Change, 1*, 1–16.

Wyrral, E. (1926). *The die-hards in the Great War Vol. I 1914–1916*. London: Harrison & Sons.

Indigenous sport and heritage: Cherbourg's Ration Shed Museum

Murray G. Phillips[a], Gary Osmond[a] and Sandra Morgan[b]

[a]School of Human Movement Studies, The University of Queensland, Queensland, Australia;
[b]Cherbourg Historical Precinct Group, Ration Shed Museum, Cherboug, Queensland, Australia

So much has been lost about the culture of Australia's Indigenous people. Their languages, traditions and heritage were dissipated under the process of white colonization from 1788. This paper investigates the actions of the people from Cherbourg, an Aboriginal settlement in southeast Queensland, Australia, to reclaim their culture, identity and heritage. The focus is specifically on the Ration Shed Museum (RSM), which officially opened in Cherbourg in 2004. The RSM is a particular type of Indigenous museum, a community museum, in which those who curate the museum are simultaneously its subjects. Through a combination of ideas drawn from new museology, critical heritage and cultural geography, the relationships between the three buildings of the museum – the Ration Shed, the Superintendent's Office and the Boys' Dormitory – and the displays of sport are examined via the voices of Cherbourg people. The buildings evoke stories of surveillance, discipline, punishment and control and, in many ways, sport mirrors these features of life at Cherbourg. Importantly, however, sport functioned in a parallel capacity by creating identity: sporting achievements were symbols of pride, resilience and hope for Indigenous people.

Introduction

The Ration Shed Museum (RSM) is situated in southeast Queensland, Australia at the predominantly Indigenous town, Cherbourg. The museum is an ongoing project that began with the relocation of a historical and culturally important building – the Ration Shed – from the periphery of Cherbourg to the center of town. The Ration Shed is a small wooden building where the Indigenous community queued weekly for decades for food rations. The first stage of the RSM was completed to coincide with the Centenary Celebrations of Cherbourg in 2004. Since that time, the RSM has been extended to include the Superintendent's Office and the Boys' Dormitory, with plans to add more structures. These buildings, as we will discuss, hold specific meanings and memories for Cherbourg people. The RSM has a number of permanent projects and exhibitions – including sport-themed displays – and it attracts a range of visitors including schoolchildren from nearby districts as well as domestic and international tourists. The Queensland Government has recognized the achievements of the RSM with the Premier's Reconciliation Award (2011) and the Gallery of Modern Art Award (2012).

We have been working in Cherbourg over several years with a particular focus on sports heritage. Our particular interest in this article is the contribution of sport to Cherbourg identity over the last century, the role of sport in the development of the RSM and the meanings associated with the specific sporting collections. To understand these issues, however, requires us to go well beyond any narrow focus on the sporting exhibitions by trying to understand the RSM as part of the contemporary museum age, as an Indigenous initiated, organized and managed museum and as a particular genre of institutionalized museums and to determine the unique features, characteristics and dynamics that have defined its past, present and possibly its future. In order to achieve this understanding, the paper will draw on knowledge associated with sport museums, the "new museology" and heritage studies.

The creation of the RSM can be understood against the much wider context of what Nora (1989) describes as sites of memory or *lieux de mémoire* – museums, archives, parades, registers and commemorative ceremonies – which exemplified the emergence of a modern historical consciousness. Not only has there been a significant increase in museums (Carson, 2008; Fyfe, 2006), but also their structure, role and function has changed: from collectors of natural history and human artifacts in the nineteenth century, museums embrace issues of national identity and social, political and cultural history including Indigenous histories (Bennett, 1995; Macintyre, 2004).

Equally importantly, the RSM can be viewed under the umbrella of collections of Indigenous artifacts and culture. These collections include both those organized by non-Indigenous and Indigenous communities. In terms of non-Indigenous communities, a host of individuals and significant state and national museums has played important roles since the early decades of the twentieth century. These individuals and institutions, nevertheless, have been criticized for failing to go beyond an anthropological framework to understand the cultures they were curating and representing. In response, these institutions created more reflective, imaginative and innovative displays (Peterson, Allen, & Hamby, 2008). The RSM is directly aligned to the second, more recent, form of collecting: Indigenous-generated endeavors that exist in many diverse arenas. Indigenous-generated collections range from storage of sacred objects in desert Australia to Indigenous keeping places and cultural centers throughout rural Australia to urban venues. In this sense, the RSM epitomizes the emergence of Indigenous generated and organized museums in the latter decades of the twentieth century and, more specifically, those Indigenous institutions that exist outside capital cities in rural areas and small towns of Australia.

Finally, the RSM is an example of a sport-related museum. Sport museums are a prominent feature of the contemporary sporting landscape and take many forms: they may be associated with professional sport teams throughout the world; colleges and universities particularly in America; specific historical sites, events and myths; and commercial enterprises (Phillips, 2012). The remit of the RSM is far broader than any of these sport-specific museums, as it is more closely aligned to other museums which focus on social, cultural, political and identity history, but recognizes the cultural significance of sport through exhibitions. As we will discuss, sporting identity and achievement have been, and continue to be, important to Cherbourg, which is reflected at the RSM.

As an Indigenous-generated and sport-related institution, we can understand more about the RSM by examining exhibition types and institutional framework variables of museums. According to Gordon (2008), museum exhibition types are academic, corporate, community, entrepreneurial or vernacular institutions and in this context the RSM is best understood as a community museum. The physical setting is a museum comprising a collection of three buildings – the Ration Shed, the Superintendent's Office and the Boys' Dormitory – some of which have been moved from their original sites in Cherbourg to create a historical precinct. The knowledge base of the RSM has been created by a mixture of academic, experiential and oral tradition knowledge forms. Academic historical knowledge has been generated by anthropologists, sociologists and historians who have written books, journal articles, government reports and theses about Cherbourg, while the lived experiences of Cherbourg's people have been preserved through material culture and recorded through oral history and memory projects. The central purpose of this museum is both to salvage the history of the town through buildings, material culture and memory and for the local community to take control of Cherbourg's heritage and history. Those charged with preserving heritage and history are all volunteers, as there are no paid staff at the museum. Local Indigenous residents and former residents, who were responsible for the establishment of the RSM in 2004, continue to drive its organization and management. These Indigenous identities have collaborated with other volunteers who have professional expertise in the fields of artistic design, film making and curating exhibitions. This combination of staff has successfully raised income from the local Cherbourg Council, the State Government and Indigenous agencies to initially create the museum and then expand the site and the exhibitions, while additional running costs are raised through venue hire, entrance fees and a gift shop.

There is one further dimension that explicitly positions the RSM as a community museum. In these types of museums, the community curates the exhibitions. As Gordon (2008) stresses, community exhibitions/museums are "produced by a person who has close personal or ancestral ties to the topic being presented. They interpret the particular history because they or their parents/grandparents/ancestors lived it" (p. 41). The RSM was created by Cherbourg elders, including Sandra Morgan, Lesley Williams and Ada Simpson. These people grew up in Cherbourg and lived under the consequences of institutionalized racism in the form of the *Aboriginals Protection Act* (1897) and subsequent iterations of this act. The Act allowed representatives of the Queensland Government to forcibly remove Indigenous people from their land to live in designated settlements. Cherbourg was one of the larger government-controlled Indigenous settlements. In all, members of at least 36 tribal groups, with diverse languages and cultures, from a jurisdiction that is two-and-a-half times larger than Texas, were forcibly removed to Cherbourg (Blake, 2001). For these reasons, Cherbourg has been described as a "total institution" designed as a form of social control over Indigenous people (Sutton, 2003).

Our key point, however, is that the RSM has resulted from "Indigenous curation" (Stanley, 2008). A defining feature of Indigenous curation is that the museum is created by those who are simultaneously its subjects. In the case of the RSM, those who generated and curate the museum also grew up and continue to live in Cherbourg. As Sandra Morgan explains: "Our dream was to create a historical site where we could tell our stories about living under the Act" (Hofmeyr & Morgan, 2009). The first-person dimension of the curatorial process, epitomized in Sandra's rationale, is philosophically and practically far removed from other museum types – particularly academic and corporate – where the museum staff, including curators, educationalists and technical staff, have little or no shared experience with the subjects of their displays. The displays and exhibitions created by museum staff in academic and corporate museums do not reflect their lived experience; at the RSM, those who are involved in the museum embody the experiences they curate.

In these ways, Gordon's typology serves the function of helping to classify the RSM as a particular form of museum and, more specifically, draws attention to the process of Indigenous curation which stresses the role of subjects as curators. Nevertheless, there is much more to understanding the RSM beyond these contributions. We look to heritage studies and the new museology to help provide a broader conceptual framework for unpacking the defining features of the RSM and its associated meanings. Heritage studies are helpful because they go beyond the institutional dimensions that sometimes limit museum studies and explore larger social, cultural, geographical and political factors. In the case of the RSM, heritage studies help focus on the role of place, space and identity (Hoelscher, 2006). The new museology draws attention to the situated and contextual meaning of material culture, the processes of commercialism and entertainment and the importance of audiences and heterogeneous responses to museums (Macdonald, 2006). Textual analysis, an important dimension of the new museology, has much to offer in understanding the narratives associated with the sport displays in the RSM.

Research for this article was conducted by Murray and Gary, as non-Indigenous academic historians, together with Sandra, as an Aboriginal elder in Cherbourg and one of the founders of the RSM, with an awareness of the principles surrounding the goal of decolonizing research (Bowechop & Erikson, 2005; Chilisa, 2012; Denzin, Lincoln, & Smith, 2008; Kovach, 2009; Rossi, Rynne, & Nelson, 2013; Smith, 1999). In particular, we were cognizant of the argument that research is "deeply embedded in the multiple layers of imperial and colonial practices" (Smith, 1999, p. 2). The ethical guidelines of the funding body for this project, the Australian Institute of Aboriginal and Torres Strait Islander Studies (AIATSIS), reflect the principles of decolonizing research and the importance of indigenous research methodologies: "At every stage, research with and about Indigenous peoples must be founded on a process of meaningful engagement and reciprocity between the researcher and the Indigenous people" (AIATSIS, 2010, p. 4). The composition of the formal collaborative team, comprising non-Indigenous and Indigenous researchers, helped in this goal. At a practical level, we structured our research in ways that aimed to be "respectful, ethical, sympathetic and useful" to Cherbourg (Smith, 1999, p. 9) and to ensure relevance to community needs, including initial consultation with the community council and RSM staff; adherence to ethical protocols; regular visits, consultation and feedback; prioritizing Indigenous voices as a way of knowing; and continuing involvement in sport history research with the RSM at their request in projects of their design.

At this point in the paper, we will introduce more voices of Indigenous people from Cherbourg. Our analysis so far has essentially been the views of Murray and Gary as historians with an interest in museology and heritage, specifically sport museums, who have attempted to comprehend the RSM as a specific form of Indigenous community museum. While this approach could be extended, we are making a narrative decision, as a central part of the history-making process informed by decolonizing research, to prioritize Indigenous voices (Forsyth, 2002, p. 74) including Cherbourg people who have written their biographies, those who have been interviewed in various oral forums and those who were responsible for the establishment of the RSM and its continuation as a functioning museum. These voices provide understanding, affective experiences and authenticity to this analysis of the RSM.

Indigenous voices, however, are rare. As one Cherbourg writer argues, this situation has resulted from "a double fold of silence. Each fold is of the same cloth – two centuries of colonisation" (Huggins & Huggins, 1994, p. 4). The first fold involves attempts to alienate Indigenous people from their culture and their history: "taking people from their lands, separating children from their parents, insisting on the surrender of traditional languages and customs and the adoption of European ways" (Huggins & Huggins, 1994, p. 4). The second fold "is the silence that you meet in Aboriginal elders who cannot bear to speak of the humiliations and mutilations they have experienced and ... witnessed" (Huggins & Huggins, 1994, p. 4). In terms of the RSM, there is a third fold. This silence is shaped by gender. Those who have written and spoken about Cherbourg are largely women; men have been reluctant to share their experiences. Stories about Cherbourg, the Ration Shed, the Superintendent's Office and the dormitories are overwhelmingly the memories of women as expressed in interviews, oral histories and autobiographies.

In order to allow Indigenous voices to speak most clearly, as historians/authors we will temporarily and partially retreat. What immediately follows is a "bricolage" created from recollections of Cherbourg residents, both past and present (Wibberley, 2012). This bricolage brings together the memories associated with the buildings of the RSM gathered from interviews, oral histories and biographies. In collecting these, we have attempted to be as comprehensive as possible, drawing upon all available records. In selectively representing these voices, we have made decisions about key themes related to the buildings and their relationship to community and individual identities. To retain authenticity as much as possible, we make no changes or corrections to grammar, punctuation or spelling. To preserve flow, we have chosen not to define key terms by parenthetically inserting definitions in the text.[1] To create a coherent narrative, we have consciously arranged the recollections with the intention of forming an ordered story (a "stained glass window"), rather than a fragmented, jarring or disjointed story (a "smashed window") (Wibberley, 2012). As this suggests, the bricolage is our construction because, as historians/authors, we make decisions about dimensions of the narrative process, specifically "who speaks and who sees" (Munslow, 2007, pp. 47–49), as well as create the subheadings of each section. This combination of Indigenous voices and authorial control is intended to help understand the role of place, space and sport in Indigenous culture and the RSM. Indigenous voices from Cherbourg appear below in relation to four topics central to the RSM: Cherbourg, the Ration Shed, the Superintendent's Office and the dormitories.

Cherbourg: removed people and forged identities

The way my mother moved around, kissed the earth and said her prayers will have a lasting effect on my soul and memory because she was paying homage and respect to her ancestors who had passed on long ago but whose presence we could both intensely feel. The land of my mother and my maternal grandmother is my land, too. It will be passed down to my children and successful generations, spiritually, in the manner that has been carried on for thousands of years. (Huggins & Huggins, 1994, p. 13)

No one had the right to remove us from our traditional lands and to do what they did to us. We were once the proud custodians of our land and now our way of life became controlled by insensitive people who know nothing about us but thought they knew everything. (Huggins & Huggins, 1994, p. 12)

Cherbourg Mission was a very depressing place to live in; our camps were so dark and miserable. There were no basic services and we had no redress through legal services to right any wrongs done to us. Who can you go to when it is the very authority set over you to govern that is committing the evil acts on you? It was a living hell here on earth. (Holt, 2001, p. 15)

No matter where I go, I will never stop going to Cherbourg. It was home to us for all those years. Not that we had a choice, of course. It was where our family was. We would have been all right anywhere as long as we had one another. (Huggins & Huggins, 1994, pp. 137–138)

Ration shed: measly offerings

The government owned a store on the reserve where an official would ration out food, clothing and blankets every fortnight, but the food was only enough to last a few days. (Huggins & Huggins, 1994, p. 19)

All the food was dried. We had split peas, sago, rice, salt, sugar, tea, flour and kerosene soap to wash with. The rations were doled out by cupfuls. You had to identify your family name and the number of people living there. You were given two cupfuls for each person and that was your entitlement for a fortnight. (Holt, 2001, p. 26)

The flour was mixed manually, the flour bags would be cut open and emptied into a wooden bin lined with tin. The bags of flour would be mixed with cream of tartar to make the flour rise. The Murries' job was to jump into the bins and mix it. With bare feet and no shirt on, on a hot day the sweat would pour from their bodies. This would all be mixed together. (Holt, 2001, pp. 26–27)

Turns out that the actual food that we received was a payment for the 32 hours work that everyone performed. (L. Williams, in Hofmeyr & Morgan, 2009)

Bags of sago, flour and rice,
Black tea, sugar, treacle oh so nice,
Green peas, yellow peas, soaked overnight,
All gathered together in a big sugar bag,
I remember going down the ration shed,
My two brothers Johnny and Red,
Mum and dad did not mind at all,
Catchin' up with family, catchin' up with friends. (Rocco, in Hofmeyr & Morgan, 2009)

Superintendent's office: the master's command post

This building here was actually the original old office. The superintendent and the other white officials controlled the settlement from this building. (L. Williams, in Hofmeyr & Morgan, 2009)

Men's roll call used to be along the fence there. Old Semple used to be there on his little stage to see that everyone was there. (E. Collins, in Hofmeyr & Morgan, 2009)

Everybody knew that the first whistle get ready, you got to get ready and get down. Second whistle you gotta be on line. Your name called out and when it's finished you gotta turn and salute the flag then. Yeah, I got six weeks for not saluting. I said, "that's not my Queen". "I'm not going to salute her". "Take him away". (Pastor H. Collins, in Hofmeyr & Morgan, 2009)

One of the blacktrackers was sent to our house asking for Harry, saying that Mr Semple had a job for him. Harry accompanied the blacktracker to Mr Semple, who told him he was going to Stanthorpe for twelve months and handed him a contract to sign. If he refused, he'd go to jail – and then be sent to Stanthorpe anyway. (Holt, 2001, p. 49)

The Government used Cherbourg as a cheap labour camp. Some of us were sent away to work on white farms, as domestics, drovers, fencers or stockmen. Others worked in industries that were set up in Cherbourg. (S. Morgan, in Hofmeyr & Morgan, 2009)

We had to go and ask the Superintendent to get married. (J. Moffatt, in Hofmeyr & Morgan, 2009)

They would come and say to you that you were wanted at the office. You knew there was something wrong. (E. Collins, in Hofmeyr & Morgan, 2009)

This was a place we were all afraid to come. Even as older people. (A. Simpson in Hofmeyr & Morgan, 2009)

Dormitories: families lost and friends made

We lived in tin huts in those days and when we got a bit older we were put in the dormitory and visited our family once a month. They took us away from our parents at 10 or 11, I don't know why. They could visit us but we couldn't go up to the camp. (Nellie Sheridan, cited in Taylor, 1988, p. 199)

These boys suffered removal from their parents as much as we did. Some of the removals were because of parents breaking up, or due to physical violence, or the kids being considered orphans by the authorities – which happened even if only one parent had died. Sometimes they were taken from their mothers even younger than girls, and put in the boys dorm at three or four. They lived by the same rules as we did. (Hegarty, 1999, p. 58)

Strict control and discipline were part of dormitory life. There was a range of chores to do such as making beds, washing clothes and linen in huge boilers, and scrubbing out the dormitory. We would go to school after breakfast and played after school. Then there were prayers, and dinner – mainly stew – which we ate in a huge dining room using enamel plates and cups. And then to bed. (Huggins & Huggins, 1994, p. 28)

Many times we were locked up in the gaol for misbehaviour, little things like being late for meals, or playing somewhere out of bounds. We would scream and yell from fear; at the same time we'd hope someone might get sorry for us and let us out. (Hegarty, 1999, p. 42)

Everyone who went through the dormitory system should be given a certificate for surviving the experience. Some may argue we were well looked after. We were fed, clothed, had a roof over our heads, but was that enough? Could this system ever take the place of loving, caring parents? It was a terrible thing to be torn away from the arms of a young mother ... (Hegarty, 1999, p. 92)

Instead of remembering what this building once stood for – order, discipline, punishment and restraint – we sensed instead the disappearance of a symbol that we once called "Home". (Hegarty, 1999, p. 140)

Reading Cherbourg recollections?

How do we understand the views of people of Cherbourg about the buildings that now represent the RSM? We propose to do this by using Harrison's (2013) view of heritage as underpinned by three key dimensions: connection, materiality and dialog. This approach enables us to engage cultural geography, particularly concepts of space and place (Mitchell, 2000), and to explore the links between heritage, cultural geography and emotions. As Harrison (2013) argues, heritage studies have

generally under-theorised the affective qualities of heritage – its materiality, the ways in which intangible heritage practices are mediated by and power distributed within interlinked webs of people and things, and the ways in which these people and things might be said to be in dialogue with one another and with the world. (p. 228)

At the RSM, the connection, materiality and dialog merge the place of Cherbourg, the buildings and its residents, past and present.

Harrison's (2013) dialogical view of heritage stresses the "relationship between people, objects, places and practices" and the "various ways in which humans and non-humans are linked in chains of connectivity, and work together to keep the past alive in the present for the future" (p. 229). It enables the investigation of Cherbourg and the associated buildings as spaces and places. de Certeau's (1984) view of space as "practiced place" has been influential in considering how human activity and experience is central to the construction of human spaces and is used by us to approach both Cherbourg and its buildings. These places, which are geographically (Cherbourg) or architecturally (buildings) static and defined, became spaces of identity. We will read these spaces through the prism of Cherbourg residents to reveal how these spaces are a "partner in a dialogue with the bodies of [residents] ... and bodies of memory" (Vertinsky & McKay, 2004, p. 5).

When the voices that describe Cherbourg as a practiced place are considered, the emotion of grief is clearly apparent. Indigenous people, under the Act, were removed from their tribal lands to several reserves in Queensland. In this sense, Cherbourg was a place, but not one of choice. People experienced a sense of loss, a sense of grief and a sense of hopelessness, about their forced removal, at the forfeiture of their tribal lands. "Place grief" is a recognized emotion, common when "we lose our home, our land, our tree-lined street" (Little, 1999, p. 91), but for Indigenous Australians, the grief is magnified. As the historian of Cherbourg explains: "unlike the European perspective ... [t]he land was sacred; it was imbued with a religious significance. The land was a source of meaning and identity" (Blake, 2001, p. 51). The grief associated with being removed from tribal lands was, and still is, palpable.

Although Cherbourg never replaced the significance of tribal lands, for several generations this "practiced place" was their home. For the various tribal groups, Cherbourg represented a new identity. This identity was forged as Indigenous languages were suppressed, customs were condemned and families were splintered; in their place, Cherbourg people were forced to engage with European culture, education and ways of life. This cultural genocide, as Blake argues: "did not leave hapless victims cultureless or bereft of identity. Despite the fragmentation of kinship networks, dislocation, and a suppression of cultural traditions, Barambah [Cherbourg] inmates retained a distinctive identity and sense of otherness" (Blake, 2001, pp. 244–245). Even though Cherbourg was a grim existence, it was home.

Cherbourg was home; a home where the Ration Shed, the Superintendent's Office and the dormitories were imbued with meaning as practiced places through daily encounters and forced internments, emotional reactions and memory (Moffatt, 2011). At Cherbourg, food was available through three avenues: from the Ration Shed, the government store and from hunting, trapping and fishing. There were many hunters and fishermen who had skills passed down from elders, but in order to pursue "bush tucker" they were required to go beyond the boundaries of the Cherbourg mission. To go hunting, trapping and fishing required a permit from the Office. Food was also purchasable from the government store, but few Indigenous people had income. The most regular and reliable food source was the Ration Shed. It was a social place where Cherbourg people worked and where they interacted as they queued for weekly or fortnightly rations. But it was a place where their plight was stark: they were dependent on the system; the food provisions were inadequate both in terms of quantity and quality with the best products and most nutritious meat reserved for the "white" people at Cherbourg; and, as was eventually realized, the food was not free at all – they worked for their rations and they paid for them through their wages which the government withheld and which have never been returned (Kidd, 2007).

The Superintendent's Office represented surveillance, discipline, punishment and control. Surveillance at roll call on each weekday as males were accounted for; discipline as they assembled in lines in the parade area and were required to salute the English monarchy; punishment when they failed to attend or if they disobeyed instructions; and control as "white" administrators sent them out to work as domestic servants, drovers, fencers or stockmen anywhere in Queensland. The Superintendent's Office – with its power to surveil, discipline, punish and control – evoked powerful emotions, most notably fear, among Cherbourg people. This might be acute fear often characterized by the hot flush, the cold tremor or the decision to run. Or it might be the type of fear that "can be a constant companion, a cast of mind, a set of the mouth" that generates "fear systems, organising our lives around prearranged signals that warn us to watch out" (Little, 1999, p. 74). When residents expressed their fear about going to the Superintendent's Office to seek permission to marry or the feelings associated with the office that have lingered for many years among the elderly, then we realize that they experienced both forms of fear.

It is fear, too, that emerges from the recollections of dormitory life. Fear that is inextricably linked to surveillance, discipline, punishment and control. Fear was generated by the Matron, a "white" government employee, who managed all aspects of the dormitories: bathing, eating, washing, schooling, recreation and punishment. Punishment was handed out for petty misbehaviors, like lateness for meals or failing to complete chores appropriately, and ranged from being whipped with a jockey's strap to the public humiliation of having your head shaved or, the most feared, being placed in the children's jail. The female children's jail was a separate building in the backyard of the girls' dormitory and it contained two small rooms for individual confinement and a larger room for multiple children. Food was bread and water and a blanket softened the floor (Blake, 2001).

Fear was accompanied by grief or maybe grief preceded fear. The grief was immediate. It was the grief of a family being separated, of children taken from their parents, with children housed in the dormitories and parents sent to work, the lucky ones working in Cherbourg, but the majority anywhere in Queensland. For parents, this evoked a sense of guilt over being unable to keep their family together, to mentor, to nurture and to provide for. For children, it was the grief associated with the loss of parents, sisters and brothers and the necessity to form new kinships with other children who often became their *de facto* families and who they shared their transition into adulthood. For both parents and children, there emerged an additional grief, after the dormitories were closed, from an appreciation of the system of structural racism imposed by the Queensland Government that rendered Indigenous people powerless.

Given the preponderance of grief, guilt and shame in the voices that describe Cherbourg, it would not be surprising if these emotions dominated the tenor of the RSM. After all, the museum was created by community members who experienced and expressed these sentiments. Nor would it be surprising if stronger emotions like anger – "aggression, hostility, rage, hate, malevolence [and] enmity" – and its pairing with fear and frustration infiltrated the museum (Little, 1999, pp. 144, 146). Anger has "personal roots, a history [and] is part of a system" and has had widespread political expression and utility for oppressed people internationally (Little, 1999, pp. 147, 160). Instead, the spirit of the museum is overwhelmingly positive while not whitewashing the negative aspects of the past, reflecting community identity through adversity and hope for future generations.

The decision to engage with positive emotions, in the context of an oppressive past, highlights a large amount of curatorial independence at Cherbourg. Unlike some other Indigenous institutions, such as the Buffalo Nations/Luxton Museum in Banff, Canada which does not own the collection it displays and where curatorial decisions require approval from a separate board, the RSM is quite independent (Mason, 2009). The curators in Cherbourg are free from any overriding administrative body to make decisions about buildings, displays and any associated narratives. The curators of the RSM, however, recognize the political and economic imperatives of managing an institution as indicated by successful applications to granting bodies, collaborations with the Cherbourg Council to achieve certain goals, and through the promotion of tourism to generate income through entry fees and the gift shop. The independence of the RSM, most notably, has given the curators – who lived through this period of history – the license to minimize the "colonial gaze" which has been commonly found in Indigenous exhibitions (Peterson et al., 2008) by creating narratives around pride, resilience and achievement that acknowledge space as "practiced place" and situate the museum in the context of present day Cherbourg.

The significance of sport

Some of the most prominent displays at the RSM are about sport. Unlike other sport museums, particularly corporate sport museums which are unashamedly celebratory (Phillips, 2012), the RSM captures some of the complexities of the relationship between sport and race addressed by scholars in many historical, political and cultural contexts (Carrington & McDonald, 2001; Hoberman, 1997; Hylton, 2008). The buildings of the RSM and associated stories, memories and artifacts provide a scaffolding to understand the institutionalized racism at Cherbourg and elsewhere in Australia. This institutionalized racism, epitomized in the consequences of various iterations of the *Aboriginals Protection Act*, limited sporting occasions to a very small sphere of life, denied opportunities as punishment for challenging the system and stereotyped Indigenous people as physically talented but incapable of functioning autonomously in society (Tatz, 1995). Yet what the RSM demonstrates and as C.L.R. James exposed so eloquently in *Beyond a Boundary*, sport can function as both a tool for colonial hegemony and dominance and a mechanism for subversion and resistance to this control (James, 1963). While sport was an activity used to exclude, punish and oppress Indigenous people in Australia, sport was simultaneously central to the formation of Aboriginal identities (Bamblett, 2009; Gorman, 2011; Hallinan & Judd, 2012; Judd, 2008; Stephen, 2010; Tatz, 2009; Tatz & Adair, 2009). The Janus face of sport – as a form of domination as well as an important instrument in identity formation – was a key feature of life at Cherbourg.

Sport, which took various forms both within the reserve and with neighboring communities, was encouraged as a "counter to idleness and vices such as gambling" (Blake, 2001, p. 224). From the early years of settlement, cricket and rugby league football emerged as popular pastimes and from the 1920s, Cherbourg teams began to compete in competition against neighboring and other regional communities. In the 1930s, the cricketers won six district championships and the football team was seldom defeated in regional competition (Blake, 2001; Cherbourg, 1979).

The success of early cricketers and footballers did more than simply provide opportunities for individual team members or episodes of entertainment and celebration for the community. As Blake has argued (2001), their "achievements helped inmates to retain a sense of dignity and self-worth in the midst of a regime that denied their humanity" (p. 231). Particular individuals helped stoke this sense of dignity and self-worth, perhaps most notably the cricketer Eddie Gilbert who in 1931 bowled the famous Australian national cricketer, Don Bradman, for no score (a "duck"). This event, which has entered Cherbourg and, indeed, national sporting folklore, had an "immeasurable effect on the settlement" (Blake, 2001, p. 227) by demonstrating to members that "black could triumph over white" and by contributing to the creation of a united people out of the many disparate tribes – "to the making of the 'one big tribe'" (Blake, 2001, pp. 227–228).

Not all individual or collective sporting experiences were liberating or positive, however. Gilbert suffered racism in several guises as a cricketer and his sporting achievements were ultimately tempered by discrimination, disappointment and despair (Colman & Edwards, 2002). The sporting career of 1930s football champion Frank Fisher (incidentally the grandfather of Cathy Freeman, 1997 and 1999 world 400-meter champion and gold medalist in the 2000 Sydney Olympic Games 400 meters) was curtailed by the superintendent. Others suffered racism, estrangement from "white" teammates and isolation in pursuing their careers. And still others, beaten down by the oppressive reserve system, lacked the self-confidence to pursue their dreams of athletic success (Bond, 2011). Despite this, sport has continued to play an important role in the social life and identity of Cherbourg to the present day, extending from cricket and football to include athletics, basketball, boxing, darts, karate, marching "girls", netball, pool, tennis and wood chopping and producing state, national and international representatives in several sports (Watkin, 2004).

Through both setback and success, sport has emerged as a potent force in shaping Cherbourg identity over time. The widespread athletic activities and range of sporting success stories gave reserve inmates and current-day residents a rare sense of control and pride that has outlasted the limited time parameters of any individual match or contest. Likewise, sport is a powerful metaphor that conjures up past injustices and symbolizes the potential for racial reconciliation. As in the previous section that aimed to elucidate the creation and meanings of place and space in Cherbourg, we will again create a bricolage to give voice to local Indigenous speakers. These voices, collected from oral history interviews, documentary sources and personal reflections exhibited in the RSM, encapsulate the place of sport in the community and help contextualize its centrality to the museum.

Sport: pride and prejudice

Sports, sports, sports, that's all we ate, and lived for. (Anonymous, in Watkin, 2004)

Those days we lived for sport. There was nothing else to do on the community. We weren't allowed off the community, unless we got a permit. Those days then, everyone was involved in sport. (H. Hegarty in Watkin, 2004)

I remember the good old days of the Cherbourg footy team, the Barambah Rovers. I started playing with them in 1928; we all played barefoot in those days. Frank Fisher was our captain for a long time; he was a good leader. Before the game he used to tell us that we weren't playing for ourselves but were playing for Cherbourg. (L. Chambers, cited in Taylor, 1988, p. 192)

Cherbourg has been noted for the many people who've played sport. They've put their name in the history books. (W.J. Stanley, in Watkin, 2004)

I think when they learn about the history more, how it was harder for our sportsmen to get where they are and they did get there because of their love of sport. There were a lot of obstacles stopping them, but they were still determined to get where they wanted to be. I reckon they are more or less unsung heroes ... For the younger people to learn too where they can be today. They haven't got the things to stop them like our people had. (S. Morgan, 2011)

Torch relay: past and present

Cherbourg voices about sport are not limited to expressions of distant memories of athletic participation and successes. Residents are proud of more recent and current sportspeople in their midst and especially of the role played by the community in two internationally significant events – the relays for the 2000 Sydney Olympic Games and the 2006 Commonwealth Games. The Sydney 2000 torch relay, in which 11,000 runners covered a 27,000 km route over 100 days through 750 towns from Uluru to the Olympic Stadium lighting by Cathy Freeman, deliberately acknowledged Indigenous Australians who strongly identified with its symbolism of ancient traditions and contemporary reconciliation of differences (Haynes, 2000; Sinclair, 2000). Cherbourg was no exception, embracing the opportunity to host a relay leg. For Cherbourg, as reflected in the voices below transcribed from plaques at the RSM in 2012, the involvement in the Olympic relay showcased local sporting achievement and transformed complex personal memories into a public expression of honor, pride and reconciliation for many participants and community members.

> For me it is an honour to share in the relaying of the Olympic Flame on its journey to Sydney. Carrying the Torch will be a once in a lifetime experience and it will be something for all to remember and share in the celebration and the spirit of reconciliation. (Patricia Bond)

> I am one very proud aboriginal woman to be running in the Olympic Torch Relay. It is a once in a lifetime honour to represent my people who I believe were deprived from showing off their sporting prowess because of prejudice and racism. (Clarissa Bligh-Malone)

> I will proudly carry the Torch for my loved ones who are near and dear to me. I will also be proud to carry the Torch for my town, Cherbourg, and all Indigenous Australians. This will be without a doubt one of the most memorable occasions of my life. (Edna Malone)

Understanding sport in the RSM

Harrison's dialogical model of heritage is again useful in understanding these multi-focal Indigenous voices about sport in Cherbourg. These voices echo, resound and reverberate through the community today and coalesce around particular individuals, events and objects represented in the RSM. These voices and their textual representation in the museum demonstrate Harrison's (2013) point that heritage is "an active assembling of a series of objects, places and practices that we choose to hold up as a mirror to the present . . . " (pp. 228–229). Currently in the RSM, this active assemblage focuses on international sporting achievements and connections forged over 50 years ago.

Following the success of 1930s era footballers and cricketers, the next wave of outstanding athletes to emerge from Cherbourg onto the national stage were the boxers Jeffrey Dynevor, Eddie Barney and Adrian Blair who represented Australia at the 1962 British Empire and Commonwealth Games (now the Commonwealth Games) in Perth, Western Australia (Tatz, 1995). Dynevor, known locally as Mitta, won gold in the bantamweight division at those games and became the first Aboriginal athlete to win a Commonwealth gold medal. Born in 1938 in western Queensland, Mitta was forcibly relocated to Cherbourg with his parents in 1946 and grew up in the boys' dormitory after his mother became ill (Morgan, 2006). His forced removal and dormitory upbringing amplified the significance of his sporting successes with locals, many of whom had shared common painful childhood experiences, and when his Empire Games triumph was announced during a movie screening in Cherbourg in late 1962 residents "clapped" and "whistled" with joy (McCutcheon, 2006).

Nearly half a century later, Mitta shared in the lighting of the cauldron for the 2000 Sydney Olympic Games torch relay leg from Cherbourg to the nearby town of Murgon. In February 2006, as part of the Melbourne Commonwealth Games, he also participated in the Queen's Baton Relay in Cherbourg, an event reported on national television (McCutcheon, 2006). The report was viewed by the wife of Mitta's coach in Cherbourg, who had possession of Mitta's boxing memorabilia and who posted the trove to him. Those items, together with the cauldron, torch, banners and official uniform from the 2000 Olympic Torch relay, now form the nucleus of the RSM's sporting and overall collection. Mitta's items include boxing singlets, shorts, shoes, gloves, shields, certificates, telegrams and news clippings complemented by posters commemorating Mitta, Blair and Barney at the 1962 British Empire Games, historic photographs and news clippings and pictures from the Olympic torch relay with testimonials from individual participants.

The local importance of the two inter-related exhibits – Mitta and the 2000 torch relay – cannot be underestimated. They combine major artifacts in a comprehensive display. They bridge the distant past with the present – a time of limited freedoms in the 1950s and 1960s with a time of greater freedoms and celebration in 2000 (Simpson, 2011). They also link past community members with current residents. And as artifacts linked to significant international events – in 1962 and 2000 – they assert community pride and provide some measure of antidote to lingering resentment, expressed in the "Voices" section above, about limited sporting opportunities in Cherbourg in the past.

As important as these displays are, other sporting items could have been used in building meaningful displays in the RSM. Mitta's belongings were a donation of serendipitous provenance and admittedly rich in content, but other exhibitions honoring any number of former sportsmen and women could have been mounted. The interconnected Mitta and Olympics collections, while varied, extensive and moving, are perhaps most important not because of their inherent worth but because they are emblematic of the place of sport in Cherbourg's living heritage. By selecting and exhibiting these exhibits, the Indigenous curators have placed "a certain construction upon history" and have imbued the objects with social importance and interpretation far beyond any meaning inherent in the objects themselves (Vergo, 1989, p. 3).

Conclusion

Through the research design, methodologies and practices, this research project achieved a significant degree of Indigenous community input into and control of the research process. As much as we attempted to approach the project through the voices of current and former Cherbourg residents, guided by Sandra, to help decolonize the research, Murray and Gary must also acknowledge that as non-Indigenous researchers we were also looking over the shoulder of these community members to make sense of the RSM. This insider/outsider dynamic is inevitable in projects like this involving non-Indigenous and Indigenous researchers and awareness of this dimension is useful for attempts by academic scholars to decolonize research (Rossi et al., 2013).

Through this process, we have understood the RSM in the context of the emergence of a modern historical consciousness and as a relatively unique community-based institution in terms of Indigenous collections and sport-related museums. We have used recollections, memories and feelings associated with the key buildings and sport exhibitions through the lenses of new museology and Harrison's version of dialogic heritage to examine meanings associated with the RSM. For us, the role of sport at the RSM is powerful. At one level, sport was a tool of institutionalized racism epitomizing limited opportunities and, at times, a form of punishment and contributing to derogatory stereotypes. Yet, at another level, sport was central to identity-making in Cherbourg. Sporting achievements were symbols of pride, resilience and hope.

Ultimately, however, the relationship between the RSM and its visitors is far more complex than we have captured. As Hooper-Greenhill (2000) has argued specifically about museums and heritage, reflecting broader debates about subjectivity, visitor impressions are shaped by personal interpretations understood within larger social and cultural interpretative frameworks. For example, what do Cherbourg children, or international backpackers, or busloads of elderly pensioners or school principals who meet every year at Cherbourg take from their visits to the RSM? Answering questions like these will provide a richer understanding of the RSM and help explore the dialogical nature of heritage that reflects the active and present-centered interrelationship between people, places and objects in the context of Cherbourg.

Note

1. Terms that may require definition are: Murries (local Aboriginal people); Semple (former Cherbourg superintendent); blacktrackers (local, Aboriginal, police force at Cherbourg); and drovers (stockmen).

References

AIATSIS. (2010). *Guidelines for ethical research in indigenous studies*. Canberra: Australian Institute of Aboriginal and Torres Strait Islander Studies. Retrieved from http://www.aiatsis.gov.au/research/docs/ethics.pdf

Bamblett, L. (2009). *Mission style: Sport and cultural continuity on erambie mission* (PhD). Charles Sturt University, NSW.

Bennett, T. (1995). *The birth of the museum: History, theory, politics*. London: Routledge.

Blake, T. (2001). *A dumping ground: A history of the Cherbourg settlement*. Brisbane: University of Queensland Press.

Bond, R. (2011). Pers. comm., October 18, 2011.

Bowechop, J., & Erikson, P. P. (2005). Forging indigenous methodologies on Cape Flattery: The Makah Museum as a center of collaborative research. *The American Indian Quarterly, 29* (1&2), 263–273.

Carrington, B., & McDonald, I. (2001). *"Race", sport, and British society*. New York: Routledge.

Carson, C. (2008). The end of history museums: What's plan B? *The Public Historian, 30* (4), 9–27.

de Certeau, M. (1984). *The practice of everyday life*. Berkeley: University of California Press.

Cherbourg Anniversary Organizing Committee. (1979). *Barambah, Cherbourg 1904–1979*. Cherbourg, Queensland: Author.

Chilisa, B. (2012). *Indigenous research methodologies*. Los Angeles, CA: Sage.

Colman, M., & Edwards, K. (2002). *Eddie Gilbert: The true story of an aboriginal cricketing legend*. Sydney: ABC.

Denzin, N. K., Lincoln, Y. S., & Smith, L. T. (Eds.). (2008). *Handbook of critical and indigenous methodologies*. Los Angeles, CA: Sage.

Forsyth, J. (2002). *Teepees and Tomahawks: Aboriginal cultural representation at the 1976 Olympic Games*. Proceedings of the sixth international symposium for Olympic research. London, ON: Centre for Olympic Studies, University of Western Ontario, pp. 71–76.

Fyfe, G. (2006). Sociology and the social aspects of museums. In S. Macdonald (Ed.), *A companion to museum studies* (pp. 33–49). Oxford: Blackwell.

Gordon, T. S. (2008). Heritage, commerce, and museal display: Toward a new typology of historical exhibition in the United States. *The Public Historian, 30* (3), 27–50.

Gorman, S. (2011). *Legends: The AFL indigenous team of the century.* Canberra: Aboriginal Studies Press.

Hallinan, C., & Judd, B. (2012). Indigenous studies and race relations in Australian sports. *Sport in Society: Cultures, Commerce, Media and Politics, 15* (7), 915–921.

Harrison, R. (2013). *Heritage: Critical approaches.* New York: Routledge.

Haynes, J. (2000). *Socio-economic impact of the Sydney 2000 Olympic Games.* Unpublished paper presented at the 2001 seminar of the International Chair in Olympism (IOC-UAB). Retrieved from http://hdl.handle.net/2072/5007

Hegarty, R. (1999). *Is that you Ruthie?* Brisbane: University of Queensland Press.

Hoberman, J. M. (1997). *Darwin's athletes: How sport has damaged Black America and preserved the myth of race.* Boston: Houghton Mifflin.

Hoelscher, S. (2006). Heritage. In S. Macdonald (Ed.), *A companion to museum studies* (pp. 198–218). Oxford: Blackwell.

Hofmeyr, R., & Morgan, S. (2009). *The ration shed [Documentary].* Cherbourg: Zebra Crossing Pictures.

Holt, A. (2001). *Forcibly removed.* Broome, WA: Magabala.

Hooper-Greenhill, E. (2000). *Museums and the interpretation of visual culture.* London: Routledge.

Huggins, R., & Huggins, J. (1994). *Aunty Rita.* Canberra: Aboriginal Studies Press.

Hylton, K. (2008). *"Race" and sport: Critical race theory.* London: Routledge.

James, C. L. R. (1963). *Beyond a boundary.* London: Hutchinson.

Judd, B. (2008). *On the boundary line: Colonial identity in football.* Melbourne: Australian Scholarly Publishing.

Kidd, R. (2007). *Hard labour, Stolen Wages: National report on Stolen Wages.* Sydney: Australians for Native Title and Reconciliation.

Kovach, M. (2009). *Indigenous methodologies: Characteristics, conversations and contexts.* Toronto: University of Toronto Press.

Little, G. (1999). *The public emotions: From mourning to hope.* Sydney: ABC.

Macdonald, S. (Ed.). (2006). *A companion to museum studies.* Oxford: Blackwell.

Macintyre, S. (Ed.). (2004). *The historian's conscience: Australian historians on the ethics of history.* Melbourne: Melbourne University Press.

Mason, C. W. (2009). The Buffalo Nations/Luxton Museum: Tourism, regional forces and problematising cultural representations of aboriginal peoples in Banff, Canada. *International Journal of Heritage Studies, 15* (4), 355–373.

McCutcheon, P. (2006, February 3). *Indigenous sporting pioneer to be honoured.* ABC TV 7.30 Report. Retrieved from http://www.abc.net.au/7.30/content/2006/s1562151.htm

Mitchell, D. (2000). *Cultural geography: A critical introduction.* Oxford: Blackwell.

Moffatt, J. (2011). *Jack's story: The life and times of a Cherbourg dormitory boy.* Taigum, Queensland: Yubuna Munya.

Morgan, S. (Director). (2006). *Up the white eyes [Documentary].* Cherbourg: Zebra Crossing Pictures.

Morgan, S. (2011). Pers. comm., February 17, 2011.

Munslow, A. (2007). *Narrative and history.* Houndmills: Palgrave Macmillan.

Nora, P. (1989). Between memory and history: Les Lieux de Mémoire. *Representations, 26,* 7–24.

Peterson, N., Allen, L. A., & Hamby, L. (Eds.). (2008). *The makers and making of indigenous Australian museum collections.* Melbourne: Melbourne University Press.

Phillips, M. G. (Ed.). (2012). *Representing the sporting past in museums and hall of fame.* New York: Routledge.

Rossi, A., Rynne, S., & Nelson, A. (2013). Doing Whitefella research in Blackfella communities in Australia: Decolonizing method in sports related research. *Quest, 65* (1), 116–131.

Simpson, A. (2011). Pers. comm., April 5, 2011.

Sinclair, J. (2000). More than an old flame: National symbolism and the media in the torch ceremony of the Olympics. *Media International Australia, 97,* 35–46.

Smith, L. T. (1999). *Decolonizing methodologies: Research and indigenous peoples.* London: Zed Books and University of Otago Press.

Stanley, N. (Ed.). (2008). *The future of indigenous museums: Perspectives from the Southwest Pacific.* New York: Berghahn.

Stephen, M. (2010). *Contact zones: Sport and race in the Northern Territory, 1869–1953.* Darwin: Charles Darwin Press.

Sutton, M.-J. (2003). Re-examining total institutions: A case study from Queensland. *Archaeology in Oceania, 38*, 78–88.

Tatz, C. (1995). *Obstacle race: Aborigines in sport*. Sydney: UNSW Press.

Tatz, C. (2009). Coming to terms: "Race", ethnicity, identity and aboriginality in sport. *Australian Aboriginal Studies, 2*, 15–31.

Tatz, C., & Adair, D. (2009). Darkness and a little light: Race and sport in Australia. *Australian Aboriginal Studies, 2*, 1–14.

Taylor, P. (Ed.). (1988). *After 200 years: Photographic essays of aboriginal and islander Australia today*. Canberra: Aboriginal Studies Press.

Vergo, P. (1989). *The new museology*. London: Reaktion.

Vertinsky, P., & McKay, S. (Eds.). (2004). *Disciplining bodies in the gymnasium*. London: Routledge.

Watkin, D. (Director). (2004). *Crossings: Passionate about sport [Documentary]*. Brisbane: Strong and Smart Foundation.

Wibberley, C. (2012). Getting to grips with bricolage: A personal account. *The Qualitative Report, 17* (50), 1–8.

Identity in the "Road Racing Capital of the World": heritage, geography and contested spaces

Ray Moore[a], Matthew Richardson[b] and Claire Corkill[a]

[a]Department of Archaeology, University of York, York, UK; [b]Manx National Heritage, Douglas, UK

This article explores the complex relationship between sport and landscape and their role in the expression and maintenance of identity. While discussions have typically emphasised the role taken by stadia and sporting venues in the development and expression of sporting and national identities, fewer have considered the role taken by the wider landscape. It is this landscape that provides the context in which many sports are enacted and watched and it is through the embodied actions and experiences that landscape is given added meaning, reinforcing narratives of space that are implicated in the creation and maintenance of national identities. Yet here, unlike stadia or other sporting venues, space is much less regulated; as a result, participants and observers are also implicated in the creation of "counter geographies" that destabilise "official" narratives of space. Here our focus is on the contested landscapes of the Isle of Man Tourist Trophy Races; an event where sporting narratives have become materially and conceptually part of the landscape. Through a discussion of these landscapes and their expression in the *Staying the Course* exhibition curated by Manx National Heritage, we contend that geographies of sport must also reflect on the contested nature of sporting spaces.

Introduction

The pervasiveness of popular culture and media throughout contemporary society has been associated with the proliferation of national identities expressed through these mediums. Arguably, its greatest expressions are seen in the increasing significance afforded to sport, sporting events, sporting venues and sporting personalities which are increasingly conceived as the ultimate demonstration of the nation, national identities and national values. Within the modern conception of nation and national identities, it is straightforward to understand how sport has become implicated. As Smith (2013) contends:

We may define the "nation" as a territorialised human community whose members share common myths and memories, a distinct public culture and common laws and customs, and "nationalism" as an ideological movement for the attainment and maintenance of autonomy, unity and identity for a human community some of whose members deem it to constitute an actual or potential "nation". (p. 88)

Underlying such a conception of nation are notions of belonging, connection and identification in which sport can be conceived as an expression of national identities. The proliferation of national identities amongst the developing urban middle class during the nineteenth century typically focused on those elements of "high" culture deemed appropriate for these intellectual élites (Smith, 1995). Consequently, behaviours and activities, like sport, construed as every day or "low" culture were marginalised (Gammon, 2007). Sports significance changed in the aftermath of the Second World War as these nineteenth century power structures disintegrated allowing the relationship between sport and identity to solidify (Smith & Porter, 2004). As one observer contends:

> At local, regional or national level, sport is, after war, probably the principle means of collective identification in modern life. It provides one of the few occasions when large, complex, impersonal and functionally bonded units such as cities or countries can unite as a whole. Identification with a sports team binds people to a place simply through ascription, an unfamiliar way of obtaining pride and status in a meritocracy. (Bale, 1986, p. 18)

Indeed, sport and sporting competition can often produce the more overt expressions of community and group identities than might otherwise be accepted within wider society and which can be readily produced and consumed by both internal and external audiences (Maguire & Tuck, 1998). Yet at the same time, sporting identities are produced and maintained spatially. As a result, sporting venues and landscapes, as socially produced spaces, are implicated in the production of ideologies and political identities. The

> practice of identity, whether national or individual, is revealed as a process in which subjectivity and identity of place are mutually constituted via bodily practice in culturally defined spaces .... Sense of place, then, is a truly lived, embodied, and felt quality of place, one that informs practice and is productive of particular representations of place. Significantly, sense of place is also an integral component of identity and psychic interiority. (Martin, 1997, p. 108)

There is no inherent identity within these spaces, instead place is constructed by human behaviour through lived experience and everyday practice. These places are not neutral and these are contested spaces where identities are brought into conflict with each other and where these identities are created and recreated through everyday existence.

It is our intention here to explore the contested relationship between sport and landscape through an exploration of the spaces of the Isle of Man Tourist Trophy (TT) Races, one of the most famous and controversial motorcycle road racing events in the world. Here we examine the relationship between the event and landscape by scrutinising the way in which the TT Races have become implicated in national identities, expressed in the embodied experience and recreated in the exhibition space.

Space, landscape and identity

While there is a long tradition of research amongst geographers and social theorists into the social construction of space, its implication in the development and maintenance of nation and national identities is a relatively recent development. Discussions treated space and landscape as primordial; an empty space in which individual, group or community was externalised where human activities were inscribed. These spaces could be inhabited, observed and changed but were not social and culturally produced spaces. More recent discussions identified space as an intrinsically sociocultural production implicated in the maintenance and promotion of élite power structures (Daniels, 1989). The subsequent reaction to this Marxist cognition of the power expressed through and within space refocused attention on those non-élites who were marginalised by such a perspective. As an autonomous space, individuals, groups and communities are free to know, acquire and participate in space. Instead, all individuals are situated in landscape and implicated in its construction, maintenance and resistance of space; here, cognitive and corporeal experience of space is influenced by and has an influence upon spaces and landscapes.

Despite this perspective discussions of nation and nationalism often marginalise space, preferring instead to foreground the primordial or ideological aspects of nation (Lefebvre, 1991). Yet, as a territorialised community, nation and nationhood are by their very nature spatial. More than this space, and particularly landscape, can contribute "to the generation of ideas of 'homeland' and national territory, as well as the related questions of ethnoscapes, 'natural frontiers' and national borders" (Smith, 2003, p. 226). British identities, for example, have created the quintessential, rural idylls which situate nation, the Scottish Highlands, the Welsh Valley's, etc. The "landscapes of the nation define and characterise the identity of its people" (Smith, 1995, p. 56).

Identities can also become embodied in the everyday habits and practices of life. These everyday activities and routines can be implicated in spatial practice and the creation of social space and relations (Lefebvre, 1991), but also in the everyday production and articulation of nation and national identities (Billig, 1995). It is through sensory and corporeal engagement with space, experiences that become embedded in memory and expressed through embodied practice and performance that place identities are created. As Bhabha (1994) contends during "the production of the nation as narration there is a split between the continuist, accumulative temporality of the pedagogical, and the repetitious, recursive strategy of the performative" (p.145). It is through the repetition of routines and habits during everyday activities and practices, and there synchronicity across space, that nation and national spaces are created.

The inherent flexibility of sport and sporting identities means that they can easily combine with other expressions of cultural identity to produce place identities (Ramshaw & Hinch, 2006). It was Bale's (1994) polemic text of the role of space and landscape which provoked discussion of the role of sport in the creation of space. Subsequent discussions of sporting spaces have typically foreground sports halls, museums and stadia arguing that they are transformed into places imbued with meaning for groups, communities and nation (Ramshaw, 2010; Wright, 2012). These venues, replete with their own internal geographies and sportscapes, can seem divorced from their surroundings and therefore dissociated from national landscapes; indeed, the globalisation of sport has led to the identification of the "placelessness" of many modern, homogenised sporting arenas (Bale, 1994). Yet despite this, these structures can become imbued with meaning from the surrounding social and cultural landscapes. Much fewer investigations have examined the role taken by sport and the wider landscape in expressions of national identity. Certainly, the image of landscape is central in sport, most notably in national sports where it has become a powerful mechanism for the expression and reproduction of identities and nationhood (Bairner, 2009). This can, at least in part, be attributed to the fact that sport allows a connection with space and place that is more readily accessible than other forms of culture. Certainly the creation of national sports, replete with nostalgic and idealised landscapes, can be central to the construction and expression of identities such as cricket in England (Bale, 2003), ice hockey in Canada (Ramshaw & Hinch, 2006) or cycling in France (Campos, 2003; Palmer, 2010).

The annual cycling event, known as the Tour de France, stands as an exemplar of how landscape and sport have become integrated in a unified expression of national identity. The "estimated five million French citizens who turn out to watch ... are well aware that they are participating in a national celebration as much as in a sporting event" (Campos, 2003, p. 171). Yet, the route taken by the race has become an equally important representation of national heritage as the simple path taken through the French landscape. The event's progress through France has become a "valorisation, above all, of the landscape" (Vigarello as cited in Palmer, 2010, p. 872). The French landscape features heavily for both competitors and spectators, from the rugged landscapes of the Alps and Pyrénées through to the châteaux of the Loire Valley and the innumerable towns and villages the race passes on its way to Paris and the Champs-Élysées. It focuses attention on the coherent and conflicting landscapes of France; constructing "an iconic reading of a 'quintessential' France" (Palmer, 2010, p. 872). Barthes (1973) has spoken of its portrayal as an epic where the "personification of nature" and the "naturalisation" of competitors' allow the event, entrants and also spectators to become part of the landscape. At the same time, more than simply marking the extent of a geographical landscape the event is also implicated in a complex negotiation with an imagined national past (Dauncey & Hare, 2003). As Palmer (2010) highlights:

> The expression of national identity through the Tour de France is done at the local and regional level. It is the piecing together of various local and regional images that together produce a sense of a unified France that has much cultural currency in discursive constructions and representations of the Tour de France. (p. 878)

At the Tour de France "the nation, sport and landscape come to be recognised as interconnected texts which taken as whole offer important insights into the formation of national identities" (Bairner, 2009, p. 236).

While the importance of motor transport to national identities is certainly well attested (Boutle, 2012; Edensor, 2004; Koshar, 2004), investigations of the role taken by motorsport are much less common. A notable exception is Dayaratne (2012) discussion of the contested landscapes of Bahrain, where contemporary purpose-built racing landscapes create an inherent tension with the grand meta-narratives of the national past. Whilst only "a handful of studies have engaged with the cultural history of motoring in Britain ... motorsport and speed records have been almost entirely ignored as areas for research" (Boutle, 2012, p. 450). An event like the Isle of Man TT Races stands as a useful exemplar where landscape, identity and motorcycle racing have become implicated in the creation and expression of distinctive national identities. Whilst discussions of the role taken by motorsport in expressions of nationhood have focused on their coherence and unitary nature, this paper aims to illustrate how such identities are challenged and destabilised through everyday activities and practice through an examination of the contested spaces and places evident throughout the Manx landscape.

The Isle of Man TT Races

With an area of only 572 km^2 and population of just over 84,000, the Isle of Man is a small nation located in the centre of the Irish Sea known for its tail-less Manx cats, its tax haven status and the unusual Three Legs of Man symbol in the centre of the Island's flag (Figure 1) (Isle of Man Government, 2013). Although a British Crown dependency, the Island has retained a strong sense of independence through self-governance in the form of Tynwald, the oldest continual parliament in the world, the retention of its own currency and the continuation of local traditions. Traditional music and dance and the recent resurgence of the Island's native language Manx Gaelic feature heavily in expressions of local identities

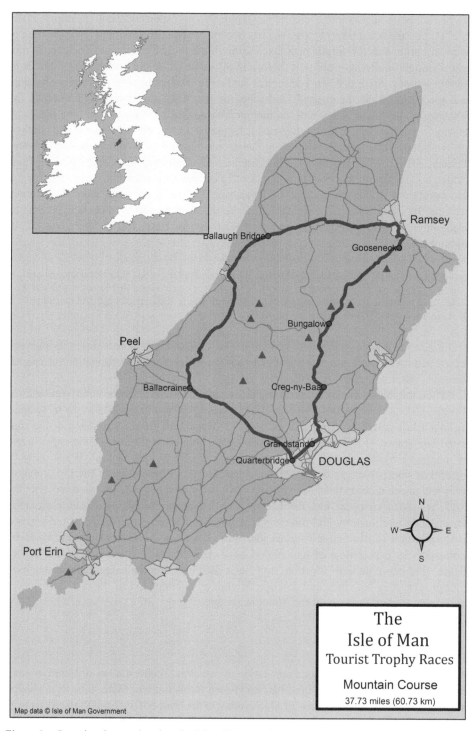

Figure 1.   Locational map showing the Isle of Man and the TT 'Mountain' Course. Map derived from the Isle of Man Survey Large Scale Base Mapping and reproduced under licence. © Crown Copyright, Department of Infrastructure, Isle of Man Government. Reproduced by permission of Department of Infrastructure.

(Thomson, 2000). With its scenic glens, numerous beaches and central upland massif, the Island's varied landscapes and natural beauty led it to become a major tourist destination for Victorian and Edwardian holiday makers (Winterbottom, 2000). Tourism remains a significant industry on the Island today, catering for smaller numbers of visitors who remain drawn by the opportunities for outdoor activities alongside cultural and heritage attractions and during late May and early June for one event in particular – the Isle of Man TT.

To many fans of the event, the Isle of Man is synonymous with the TT with the Island known as both the "Road Racing Capital of the World" (Duckworth, 2007, p. 3) and the "Mecca of Motorcycling" (Hoskin, 2006). For two weeks of the year tens of thousands of dedicated fans flock to watch a week of practicing, followed by four days of racing, but also to take their own turn around the course when the roads reopen. As the British round of the FIM Motorcycle Grand Prix World Championship (1949–1976), the event blossomed into one of the most popular events in the series, but the removal of World Championship status, due to worries over safety, saw an almost terminal decline in visitors during the late 1970s and 1980s. The support from the road racing community with the backing of the Isle of Man Government saw the event continue and regain popularity. A 2010 survey reported that the TT Races attracted some 31,000 visitors (Isle of Man Government, 2010), but numbers have risen substantially in recent years as a consequence of a publicity campaign from the Isle of Man Government and the release of the film *TT3D: Closer to the Edge* (2011).[1] The TT also received some 400 hours of global TV coverage, with UK coverage by ITV4 attracting audiences in excess of 8.5 million viewers for its 14 programmes and the event's official website reported over 1.5 million visits, with large numbers following on social media (Anonymous, 2012).

First staged in 1904, the TT has been run annually ever since. Initially an event for motorcars developed by the Automobile Club of Great Britain and Ireland as part of the Gordon Bennet Cup, it comprised a series of time trials held over the Island's public roads (Duckworth, 2007; Faragher, 2000). The following year racing was once again held, but this time moving from the 52 mile course running between Castletown and Ramsey to a shorter 15 and a half miles on the St John's, or Short Course, located in the west of the Island (Wright, 2007). The same year (1905) also saw the introduction of a motorcycle race which acted as a qualifier for the International Cup. Inspired by this and spurred on by the competitor's subsequent lack of success in international events, the Auto Cycle Club began to organise a new event designed to inspire British manufacturers to increase the reliability and speed of their machines. This event was to be the Isle of Man TT, and 1907 saw Charlie Collier take victory in the inaugural race, with an average speed of 38.22 mph (Wright, 2007). In 1911 the races were held for the first time on the new 37.73 mile Mountain Circuit which included a challenging 1400 ft climb up Snaefell, the Island's only mountain (Wright, 2007). The next major development came in 1949 when the event was made part of the newly founded FIM World Championships (Anonymous, 2010). This status drew some of the world's greatest riders to the TT from six-time World Champion Geoff Duke to the legendary Mike Hailwood and Giacomo Agostini (Anonymous, 2010).

Improvements to both machine and track over time have seen dramatic developments in the speeds riders can accomplish. With top speeds in excess of 200 mph John McGuinness holds the current lap record of 17 m 12.3 s (an average speed of 132/212 kph) (Corkill & Moore, 2012). With such high speeds come inevitable dangers and the implications of crashing on public roads can be fatal. The death of Yoshinari Matsushita, following a crash at Ballacrye during practicing for the 2013 races, marked the 240th death in the event's history (Anonymous, 2013). Whilst the biking community applies heroic status to the riders who take part, such as the iconic "King of the Mountain" Joey Dunlop, holder of a record of 26 TT wins, discussion in wider arenas frequently focuses on the dangers of the sport. While media reports on race results are often minimal, articles detailing serious incidents and fatalities tend to receive greater prominence boosted by dramatic headlines such as the Daily Mail's 2003 article titled "How Many More Will have To Die?" (Woolridge, 2003; see also Corkill & Moore, 2012). The riders themselves are more than aware of the consequences they may face, none more so than David Jefferies, who prior to his death racing in the TT in 2000 stated "To succeed on the Island you have to be totally at ease with yourself, know what you are doing and accept that you might be going home in a box" (Gillan, 2005, p. 6).

The release in 2011 of the film *TT3D: Closer to the Edge* (2011) which followed contemporary riders preparing for, and during, the 2010 event marked a new era in the portrayal of the TT races. Whereas previous documentaries were designed for those with a specific interest in motor racing, focusing on the machinery and the race coverage, *TT3D: Closer to the Edge* drew on the experiences of riders such as Guy Martin, Ian Hutchinson and John McGuinness and while not shirking away from the dangers involved highlighted their skill, commitment, humanity and even humour making the event accessible to a much wider audience. The cinematography used within the film situates the viewer, the riders and its spectators in the Manx landscape, locating and placing the event spatially. *TT3D* also serves to illustrate how these riders and their narratives have become implicated in creation of community identities, drawn together and expressed within the Manx landscape.

Sport, heritage and place at the Isle of Man TT Races

Rural landscapes feature heavily in the creation and maintenance of identities in the Isle of Man. The Manx National Glens, for example, have come to be regarded as a "treasured landscape", "not necessarily in the sense of formal conservational importance or spatial designation, but in terms of popular consciousness and identity" (Prentice, 1992, p. 127). While concerns over the appropriate use of the uplands attest to the significance of this environment (Turner, 2013), cultural and historical landscapes, such as the remote upland community at Cregneash (now preserved as an open-air Folk Museum), also feature in these identities. Here, the village replete with thatched cottages, traditional crofting activities and Manx speaking guides (re-)presents a vision of traditional rural life. As a venue for the revitalisation of traditional practices, calendar customs, language and dance, Cregneash lends authenticity to these cultural revival activities. While Cregneash presents a "living" rural culture, the Manx landscape is also littered with ruined farms and houses, known locally as *tholtans*. These structures serve as allegories to the state of Manx culture "not as a dead pile of stones, but as an evocative, rather poetic reminder of life's processes" (Lewis, 2012, p. 102; Maddrell, 2006). These picturesque locales and rural idylls have become the quintessential Manx landscapes, not simply a backdrop, but a defining feature for Manx culture. Outwardly, there seems an incongruent tension between these natural and cultural landscapes, integral to Manx identities, and the TT Races, where "[w]hizzing iron monsters may be perceived ... as forceful contaminators of an imagined picturesque, serene and virginal landscape" (Crowther, 2007). Indeed, this very conflict is played out visually in the opening scenes of the film *TT3D: Closer to the Edge* (2011) where a peaceful rural idyll is shattered by a speeding motorbike. A cursory examination would certainly suggest some discordance, when in reality the races are as embedded in the sublime as the Manx glens, bays and tholtans; the event is implicitly connected to these idealised rural landscapes. The film *TT3D: Closer to the Edge* (2011) serves to illustrate this, peppered as it is with imagery that firmly situates competitors, spectator, the viewer and the event itself within the wider Manx landscape. The film represents the most recent expression of an imagery which can be traced deep into the events history, which pictured competitors at the courses iconic locales; the TT Grandstand, Ballaugh Bridge or Creg ny Baa. It is this relationship between the TT Races and the landscape which plays an important role not only in the reading and perception of the landscape, but also more broadly in the reading of Manx identity. In recent years this distinction has often been exaggerated within the tourist literature as a mechanism to conceptually separate what are perceived as two discrete tourist markets – the motorsport fan and the cultural tourist. These seemingly contested landscapes seem incongruent, but in reality are implicated in the routine experiences of the Manx countryside.

The embodied practice of the TT Races extends far beyond the traditional competitor and spectator relationship. The event relies heavily on the involvement of an army of local volunteers to carry out many of the duties of running a large event. This activity brings together diverse, and often discursive, factions of the local community where they become implicated in the creation, representation and reinforcement of identities. Within a community where some 52% of the population were born elsewhere (Isle of Man Government, 2012), the TT can be regarded as one of a handful of events which brings together the population and cements community bonds. At the same time as an event run over public roads the very act of travelling through the Manx landscape serves as embodied reiteration of race narratives; through these actions the event is introduced into everyday experience and discourse. As Crowther (2007) contends:

> New symbolic meanings and place myths have emerged out of the embodied practices … established by the place, where action, adventure, fun, sensation, excitement, supply mythical elements to an audience eager to explore personal capacity for adaptive performance.

Like other narratives in the Manx landscape, those of the TT "are communicated through the tales told in the car or around the table, involving movement between places, or the physical sensations association with being in places" (Lewis, 2012, p. 102). Naming plays an important role in the creation of the TT landscape infusing it with cultural meaning and social power and transmuting space into places that can be discovered and understood. Within the TT landscape, place names are literally written into the landscape through the orange and white boards which demarcate the route of the course (Figure 2). From a utilitarian perspective these signs provide spatial orientation for locals, competitors and visitors, but they also "have a semantic depth that extends beyond the concern with simple reference to location" (Entrikin, 1991, pp. 55–56). Serving as aide-mémoire these names introduce racing geographies and histories into shared cultural experience. Some of the place names memorialise the event's heroes, acting as allegories for achievement and introducing narratives of accomplishment and victory. Place names dedicated to five-time world champion, Mike Hailwood (Hailwood's Height and Hailwood's Rise) situates one of the event's most popular and successful competitors in the wider TT landscape. The positioning of these names at the highest points on the course reinforcing messages of accomplishment and triumph, a rider notionally and tangibly placed at the pinnacle of TT history and landscape (Figure 3). Similarly, Joey Dunlop the event's most successful competitor is commemorated at "Joey's", a right hand corner at the course's 26th Milestone. His 26 TT victories reiterated figuratively and literally as a milestone in the event's history. Such use of personal names is firmly entrenched within the Manx nomenclature; indeed,

Figure 2.   Marking place in the TT landscape at Ballaugh Bridge, Isle of Man. © Ray Moore.

Figure 3.   Placing riders in the TT landscape at Hailwood Heights, Isle of Man. © Ray Moore.

amongst the local population surnames provide a mechanism for situating and contextua-
lising the individual (Lewis, 2012). The commemoration of these individuals performs a
similar function, locating them in the TT landscape and its history.

As the event has struggled against negative publicity within the national and international media, the local administration has become more selective in which narratives should be remembered and which should be forgotten. While they are keen to assert the heritage of the event and the challenges of racing a motorcycle at speeds in excess of 200 mph (322 kph) along a course which passes within inches of street furniture, stone walls and houses, they have been somewhat indifferent to the inherent dangers and threat to life which the races pose. As two of the authors have stated elsewhere:

> Death at the TT Races remains the "elephant in the room", rarely openly discussed, often hidden from view, seldom debated within 'official' or documentary sources and under no circumstances publicized in histories or heritage displays. (Corkill & Moore, 2012, p. 259)

This innate tension is implicated in the production of contested spaces and places within the Manx landscape as narratives of death are marginalised in favour of those which emphasise triumph and success. The outcome of this has seen a "toponymic cleansing" of the TT landscape where those names and narratives associated with death and fatality are being increasingly written out of the landscape. Birkin's Bend, for example, which commemorated Charles "Archie" Birkin who was killed at the corner in 1927, survived for some 70 years within reports, maps and the wider landscape before reverting to its original name, Rhencullen in the late 1990s. Similarly, Horn's Corner and Drinkwater's Bend have reverted to their original names Laurel Bank and the 11th Milestone. Such "official" forgetting of narratives of death have been negated amongst spectators, marshals and the local community where these place names continue to be used, with the associated narratives recalled. The creation of these "counter geographies" serves to disrupt the homogenous, imagined spaces created by race organisers.[2] The result has been production of a sanitised TT landscape that negates the negative narratives and sentiments that these place names imbue. As Dayaratne (2012) contends:

> Spaces of national representation and spatial representations of nations are often at odds with each other. Nationalism has become and remains a signification of this conflict: the form of top-down homogenization of a people living in a particular territory ... landscapes can themselves constitute conflicting symbolisms, created by the state and the people who may have differing conceptualizations of their national identities. (p. 310)

These place names perform both a denoted and connoted function. As such then, they represent and re-present the individuals they commemorate, imbuing the wider landscape with a broad spectrum of racing and personal narratives that are experienced in the everyday. Through the very action of reading and speaking these place names, individuals and narratives are appropriated and reintroduced into the present (Basso, 1988). This action similarly enforces an innate connection between the event, the individual and landscape by promoting a sense of belonging and familiarity. The result is "powerful semiotic texts embedded in larger systems of meaning and discourse that are read, interpreted, and acted upon socially by people in different ways" (Rose-Redwood, Alderman, & Azaryahu, 2010, p. 458). As Vaukins (2007) observes, "people cannot forget that the Isle of Man is the venue for the TT. Residents are reminded of this every day. *The TT is written into the landscape*" (2007, our emphasis). Yet this

> space is becoming increasingly constrained as visits become progressively more choreographed by a government see[k]ing to attract international capital .... Marketers have exploited mythic fantasies that relate to enduring narratives of heroic encounters by racers

such as Mike Hailwood and Joey Dunlop in the epic setting of the Isle of Man. (Crowther, 2007)

Each year more areas of the course are closed to spectators (albeit in the name of safety), temporary grandstands are erected in particular locations and official guides promote places and particular locations as the quintessential TT experience. Yet, such proscribed experiences are regularly subverted by racing and the local communities as individuals annually return to favoured places to watch the racing; driven by tradition, nostalgia and a desire to recreate the first TT experience. For spectator and official alike, the landscape has become a contested space.

Embedded in motorcycling heritage, history plays an important role in the success and the continued popularity of the TT Races. In 2007 the TT Races celebrated their centenary, a milestone in the history of the event. With the anniversary on the horizon *Manx National Heritage* (MNH), the government agency responsible for the protection, preservation and promotion of the cultural and historical heritage of the Isle of Man (Manx National Heritage, n.d.) committed itself to marking the centenary with a major temporary exhibition, entitled *Staying the Course* (Figure 4). Influenced by the TT Races' position as a community event, the approach adopted within the exhibition differed radically from that adopted in other motorcycle and sporting museums in that it focused on the people who made the event happen (Manx National Heritage, 2007). The exhibition used material culture as symbolic signposts to introduce personalities and present narratives, included the narratives of marshals, spectators and manufacturers. This stands in marked contrast to usual treatment of sporting exhibitions which have tended to focus on iconic sports personalities and heroes or include facts and figures about events and collections which are passively consumed (Ramshaw, 2010). Instead, the primary focus of the exhibition is not the object per se but the wider history and narrative which it has come to signify. These individuals spoke directly as themselves, rather than being presented in the third person as the subject of an editorial process mediated by museum professionals. While the exhibition reflects wider changes in the profession as:

> Increasingly those employed or engaged in heritage management practice see the past as something we (society) actively engage with, not something only a select group of heritage managers pontificate upon and "manage". That's what the heritage should be about: the everyday, the everywhere and something for (and of) everybody. (Schofield, 2006)

The approach served to emphasise the notion that the TT Races are a community event in which different and disparate individuals and groups participate. Any relationship was reinforced by the approach adopted during the creation of the exhibition; where MNH purposefully solicited the involvement of local and racing communities in the collection of material culture and narratives, each united by a commitment to the history and heritage of the event and who wished to see it celebrated. That this appeal elicited such a wide variety of material culture, much of which would later feature in the exhibition and spanning the full history of the TT, illustrated both the significance of the event and also the "power" that such community engagement can solicit. Like other exhibitions "[c]aptured within the walls of museums and on the panels of exhibitions, the synergies between community and heritage are concentrated" (Crooke, 2010, p. 27).

Significantly, *Staying the Course* also became a space for the expression of counter narratives of the TT Races. Arguably its most poignant display was a burned out sidecar; this object was emblematic of the narrative of sidecar legend Dave Molyneux who had narrowly

Figure 4. The *Staying the Course* exhibition. © MNH. Reproduced by permission of Matthew Richardson.

survived the crash in which the machine was destroyed. The sidecar was displayed alongside a collection of trophies and a video interview of him discussing his philosophy. This part of the exhibition captured the determination required to become a successful racer, the glory that racers strive to achieve, but at the same time highlighted the terrible risks and dangers which come with the pursuit of glory (Manx National Heritage, 2007). Much like the "counter geographies" and contested spaces found in the wider landscape, the *Staying the Course* exhibition allowed the presentation of narratives that opposed traditional readings of the event. Here,

[r]ather than being perceived as remains of a lost past, certifying its demise, museum objects are considered to be the material hinges of a potential recovery of shared meanings, by means of narrativization and performativity. By granting a voice to what has been left out of the dominant discourses of history, diverse and sometimes even incompatible narratives have supposedly been granted a locus in a museal space that claims to aspire no longer to any totalizing synthesis, but to a mode of representation that has so far been the domain of art, film and literature. (Arnold-de Simine, 2012, p. 17)

Staying the Course became an expression of the TT landscape in microcosm; here space became place, narratives were signposted within the exhibition space through the use of material culture. Montages of archive and contemporary imagery and video footage allowed the recreation of the landscape, allowing visitors to experience the disparate strands of the TT landscape which would otherwise only be encountered in palimpsest. Discussing MNH's mandate, Harrison (2002) observes "the whole of the community landscape should be the subject of the 'museum' presentation" (p. 356).

The exhibition proved extremely popular. During its first two weeks, it attracted some 17,500 visitors and continued to draw good audiences throughout the summer of 2007; indeed, it was so popular that it was extended for two months beyond to service the local population outside the tourist season (Manx National Heritage, 2008). Reaction from amongst the local audience was especially positive, leading many to reaffirm what a unique event the TT Races are, how incredibly fortunate the Isle of Man was that it had survived and how the Island should make more of this asset (Richardson, cited by Isle of Man Government, n.d.). This popularity serves to illustrate the importance of the event to both local and racing communities. Hosted in the *MNH Museum*, the "Treasure House of the Isle of Man",[3] the symbolic "home" of Manx history gave this narrative a sense of authenticity. Here the role of the museum as a powerful tool in legitimising and reinforcing identities is clearly evidenced (Ramshaw & Gammon, 2010), but more than this the *Staying the Course* exhibition is indicative of the innate tensions within and between these identities. The exhibition hall, much like the wider landscape, has become a contested space where these tensions are made manifest.

Conclusion

That the TT Races are an important part of the Manx consciousness cannot be doubted; indeed, for "a large majority of residents ... the races create a national feeling ... and are part of the Island's twentieth century heritage" (Prentice, 1988, p. 156). At the same time, the traditional discussions of Manx identities have focused on the role taken by cultural revival and survival movements that developed as a consequence of the burgeoning local middle class during the late nineteenth century (Belchem, 2000; Maddrell, 2006). Within these fledgling identities, sport was often regarded with some diffidence; writing at the close of the nineteenth century one local antiquarian remarked "[t]here is nothing peculiar about the outdoor games of either young or grown-up Manxmen and Manxwomen, and they are, therefore, of little interest" (Moore, 1891, p. 179). Sport now takes an increasingly important role in expressions of national identity in the Isle of Man. The successes of cyclists Mark Cavendish (Road Racing World Champion in 2011) and Peter Kennaugh (Olympic Gold medallist in 2012) have raised the profile of the Manx sport to international audiences and have seen the sport become a defining feature of local identities. The TT Races have also become "ingrained within Manx identity" (Vaukins, 2007). Judging when the TT Races rose to prominence is difficult to pinpoint, but probably developed from the adverse publicity within the national and international press and repeated calls for the event to be cancelled (Vaukins, 2007). It is this fervent defence which has united the diffuse racing and resident communities and implicated the TT Races in expressions of collective identities. This pressure from without has led local authorities to promote a coherent, carefully constructed official narrative of the TT Races that marginalises those aspects considered detrimental to the event's image. This constrained portrayal has increasingly estranged many of those for whom the event has become integral to individual or collective identities. These innate tensions are made manifest in the Manx landscape through the production of counter spaces and alternative geographies, reflected in place names and death memorials created by competitors, spectators and the local community. At the same time, the *Staying the Course* exhibition certainly serves to demonstrate how,

> re-creating sporting pasts for a tourist audience, nostalgic depictions serve to articulate what a region or a nation believes is important about its sporting past. In doing so, the destination is constructing its place identity. (Ramshaw & Hinch, 2006, p. 400)

The TT Races are obviously important to these place identities; the success of the *Staying the Course* exhibition amongst visiting and particularly local communities attests to its salience. Within the current milieu, "sport heritage is imagined largely within the parameters offered by its tourism potential and output" (Gammon, Ramshaw, & Waterton, 2013, p. 120) and this is certainly evidenced in previous discussions of the TT Races (Prentice, 1988). The role of MNH in articulating and promoting cohesive identities, which promote internal stability and national pride, is clearly evidenced within other heritage presentations (Isle of Man Government, 1999; Lewis, 2006). The *Staying the Course* exhibition serves as a somewhat atypical example of how the contested nature of identities can be represented and replayed in the exhibition hall. As Ramshaw (2010) observes, sporting exhibitions often seek to "venerate and celebrate athletes, teams or past achievements" (pp. 49–50) and this is something that is certainly evidenced in the *Staying the Course* exhibition. Yet the exhibition also serves as an exemplar of how heritage agencies can play an important role in the creation and portrayal of alternative narratives; creating a contested space that can highlight and engage with the innate tensions between these and official identities and spaces. While material culture remains at the very heart of the *Staying the Course* exhibition, the choice of objects is often less obvious. In discussing the career of sidecar rider Dave Molyneaux, curators could have easily chosen a trophy or winning machine, but instead exhibited an alternative narrative represented by the machine he crashed during the 2006 event. Such an object highlighted the associated dangers and threat of injury that the TT Races bring, something that is rarely openly acknowledged and often marginalised within official accounts of the event and any associated identities. Here within the exhibition space the fragmented narratives of the TT Races are brought together. Of course these accounts invariably contradict official histories and identities, but the exhibition makes no attempt to disguise this ambiguity. Even here the selection of narratives was carefully considered and managed. Unlike so many Molyneaux had survived his accident; his was a survivor narrative. Again accounts of death, and those killed whilst participating in the event, were marginalised. Instead, these narratives are played out in the Manx landscape where individuals and groups have much more freedom to express alternative readings of the event. While these narratives are more subtle, indeed in some circumstances have been purposefully hidden (Corkill & Moore, 2012), they can still be read and implicated in wider collective identities. There intrinsic power develops from the fact that they can be experienced in the everyday. In some circumstances, these narratives may be signified through a physical presence (e.g. death memorials), but in other instances have a more limited corporeal, but equally powerful presence (e.g. place names). It is hoped that we have shown that both the exhibition space and the landscape are contested spaces where narratives, histories and identities collide and are played out.

The Isle of Man TT Races serve as a useful example in addressing "modern sports disregard of the natural landscape" (Bale, 1994, p. 10). Discussions of contested spaces within sports heritage have focused on the roles discrete sporting spaces, heritage displays and landscapes can take in the creation of place and identities (e.g. stadia, museums, etc.). Here our focus has been on the role taken by the landscape and place in the creation of sports heritage in the maintenance of collective identities (Bairner, 2009). Moving beyond the usual concerns with the materiality of sports heritage, we suggest that object, place and landscape are all implicated in the creation and maintenance of complex narratives that embody nation, but which also offer opportunities to subvert and undermine official narratives and expressions of heritage. The transient subtlety of these narratives means that they are more difficult to observe within discussions of sporting heritage, but we would suggest that they are still worthy of study.

Notes

1. In 2012, 35,172 passengers and 11,237 motorcycles travelled by ferry to the Isle of Man between 23 May and 8 June, a 16.7% increase since 2009 (BBC News, 2012).
2. These counter geographies are similarly manifest in the memorials raised to those killed whilst participating or spectating in the event (Corkill & Moore, 2012; Moore & Corkill, 2012).
3. "Thie Tashtee Vannin", the literal translation of the Manx Gaelic for museum.

References

Anonymous. (2010). *The history of the TT.* Retrieved September 12, 2013, from http://www.iomtt.com/History.aspx

Anonymous. (2012). Growth of Isle of Man TT continues with increased audience, visitors and income. Retrieved September 12, 2013, from http://www.iomtt.com/News/2012/10/25/Growth-of-Isle-of-Man-TT-continues-with-increased-audience-visitors-and-income.aspx

Anonymous. (2013, May 28). Motorcycling; Sport in brief. *The Daily Telegraph*, p. 15.

Arnold-de Simine, S. (2012). Memory museum and museum text intermediality in Daniel Libeskind's Jewish Museum and W.G. Sebald' Austerlitz. *Theory, Culture & Society, 29*(1), 14–35. doi:10.1177/0263276411423034

Bairner, A. (2009). National sports and national landscapes: In defence of primordialism. *National Identities, 11*(3), 223–239. doi:10.1080/14608940903081101

Bale, J. (1986). Sport and national identity: A geographical view. *International Journal of the History of Sport, 3*(1), 18–41. doi:10.1080/02649378608713587

Bale, J. (1994). *Landscapes of modern sport.* Leicester: Leicester University Press.

Bale, J. (2003). *Sports geographies.* London: Routledge.

Barthes, R. (1973). *Mythologies.* London: Paladin.

Basso, K. H. (1988). Speaking with names: Language and landscape among the western Apache. *Cultural Anthropology, 3*(2), 99–130. doi:10.1525/can.1988.3.2.02a00010

BBC News (2012, June 9). Isle of Man Isle of Man TT sees rise in visitor numbers. *BBC News.* Retrieved September 13, 2013, from http://www.bbc.co.uk/news/world-europe-isle-of-man-18379312

Belchem, J. (2000). The little Manx Nation: Antiquarianism, ethnic identity, and home rule politics in the Isle of Man, 1880–1918. *Journal of British Studies, 39*(2), 217–240. Retrieved from http://www.jstor.org/stable/175939

Bhabha, H. (1994). *The location of culture.* London: Routledge.

Billig, M. (1995). *Banal nationalism.* London: Sage.

Boutle, I. (2012). 'Speed lies in the lap of the English': Motor records, masculinity, and the nation, 1907–14. *Twentieth Century British History, 23*(4), 449–472. doi:10.1093/tcbh/hwr068

Campos, C. (2003). Beating the bounds: The Tour de France and national identity. *International Journal of the History of Sport*, *20*(2), 149–174. doi:10.1080/09523360412331305673

Corkill, C. & Moore, R. (2012). 'The Island of Blood': Death and commemoration at the Isle of Man TT Races. *World Archaeology*, *44*(2), 248–262. doi:10.1080/00438243.2012.669642

Crooke, E. (2010). The politics of community heritage: Motivations, authority and control. *International Journal of Heritage Studies*, *16*(1–2), 16–29. doi:10.1080/13527250903441705

Crowther, G. (2007). Embodied experiences of motorcycling at the Isle of Man TT Races. *International Journal of Motorcycle Studies*, *3*(3). Retrieved September 12, 2013, from http://ijms.nova.edu/November2007TT/IJMS_Artcl.Crowther.html

Daniels, S. (1989). Marxism, culture, and the duplicity of landscape. In R. Peet & N. Thrift (Eds.), *New models in geography*. (pp. 196–220). London: Unwin Hyman.

Dauncey, H. & Hare, G. (2003). The Tour de France: A pre-modern contest in a post-modern context. *International Journal of the History of Sport*, *20*(2), 1–29. doi:10.1080/09523360412331305613

Dayaratne, R. (2012). Landscapes of nation: Constructing national identity in the deserts of Bahrain. *National Identities*, *14*(3), 309–327. doi:10.1080/14608944.2012.702744

Duckworth, M. (2007). *TT 100. The official authorised history of the Isle of Man Tourist Trophy Racing.* Isle of Man: Lily.

Edensor, T. (2004). Automobility and national identity: Representation, geography and driving practice. *Theory, Culture and Society*, *21*(4–5), 101–120. doi:10.1177/0263276404046063

Entrikin, J. N. (1991). *The betweenness of place: Towards a geography of modernity*. Baltimore: Johns Hopkins Press.

Faragher, M. (2000). Cultural history: Motor-cycle road racing. In J. Belchem (Ed.), *A new history of the Isle of Man, Vol. 5, The modern period 1830–1999* (pp. 410–416). Liverpool: Liverpool University Press.

Gammon, S. (2007). Introduction: Sport, heritage and the English. An opportunity missed? In S. Gammon & G. Ramshaw (Eds.), *Heritage, sport and tourism: Sporting pasts – tourist futures* (pp. 1–9). London: Routledge.

Gammon, S., Ramshaw, G., & Waterton, E. (2013). Examining the olympics: Heritage, identity and performance. *International Journal of Heritage Studies*, *19*(2), 119–124. doi:10.1080/13527258.2012.687395

Gillan, A. (2005, June 4). Twists, turns and death round every bend. *The Guardian*, p. 6.

Harrison, S. (2002). Culture, tourism and local community – The heritage identity of the Isle of Man. *Journal of Brand Management*, *9*(4/5), 355–371. doi:10.1057/palgrave.bm.2540083

Hoskin, S. (2006). *The Mecca of motorcycling*. Retrieved September 12, 2013, from http://www.pukeariki.com/Research/Taranaki-Research-Centre/Taranaki-Stories/Taranaki-Story/id/625/title/the-mecca-of-motorcycling

Isle of Man Government. (1999). *The 1999 Policy Review Volume 2: Departmental service headings*. Douglas: Isle of Man Government.

Isle of Man Government. (n.d.). *'Staying the Course' stays on!* Retrieved September 8, 2013, from http://www.gov.im/RTLC/ViewNews.gov?page=lib/news/mnh/stayingthecourse1.xml&menuid=11570

Isle of Man Government. (2010). *TT Survey 2010*. Douglas: Isle of Man Government. Retrieved September 12, 2013, from https://www.gov.im/media/219411/tt_survey_report_2010.pdf

Isle of Man Government. (2012). *Isle of Man Census Report 2011*. Douglas: Isle of Man Government. Retrieved September 12, 2013, from http://www.gov.im/media/207882/census2011reportfinal resized_1_.pdf

Isle of Man Government. (2013). Island facts. Retrieved September 12, 2013, from http://www.gov.im/isleofman/facts.xml

Koshar, R. (2004). Cars and nations: Anglo-German perspectives on automobility between the world. *Theory, Culture and Society*, *21*(4–5), 121–144. doi:10.4135/9781446212578

Lefebvre, H. (1991). *The production of space*. Oxford: Blackwell.

Lewis, S. (2006). The story of Mann and all that, or how heritage became history again. *Celtic Cultural Studies*. Retrieved September 8, 2013, from http://www.celtic-cultural-studies.com/papers/05/lewis-01.html

Lewis, S. (2012). Thalloo My Vea: Narrating the landscapes of life in the Isle of Man. In A. Árnason, N. Ellison, J. Vergunst & A. Whitehouse (Eds.), *Landscapes beyond land: Routes, aesthetics, narratives* (pp. 98–115). Oxford: Berghahn.

Maddrell, B. (2006). Of demolition and reconstruction: A comparative reading of Manx cultural revivals. *e-Keltoi: Journal of Interdisciplinary Celtic Studies, 2*, 133–163. Retrieved from http://www4.uwm.edu/celtic/ekeltoi/volumes/vol2/2_4/maddrell_2_4.pdf

Maguire, J., & Tuck, J. (1998). Global sports and patriot games: Rugby union and national identity in a united sporting kingdom since 1945. In M. Cronin & D. Mayall (Eds.), *Sporting nationalisms: Identity, ethnicity, immigration and assimilation* (pp. 103–126). London: Frank Cass.

Manx National Heritage. (2007). *Staying the course. A special exhibition celebrating the people who have made the TT.* Douglas: Manx National Heritage.

Manx National Heritage. (2008). *Manx national heritage annual review: April 2007 to March 2008.* s.l.: unpublished.

Manx National Heritage. (n.d.). *Our mission.* Retrieved September 8, 2013, from http://www.manxnationalheritage.im/what-we-do/our-mission/

Martin, A. K. (1997). The practice of identity and an Irish sense of place. *Gender, Place & Culture: A Journal of Feminist Geography, 4*(1), 89–114. doi:10.1080/09663699725512

Moore, A. W. (1891). *The folk-lore of the Isle of Man: Being an account of its myths, legends, superstitions, customs, and proverbs.* Douglas: Brown

Moore, R., & Corkill, C. (2012). *Memorials from the Isle of Man TT Races.* Retrieved September 8, 2013, from http://dx.doi.org/10.5284/1016122

Palmer, C. (2010). 'We close towns for a living': Spatial transformation and the Tour de France. *Social & Cultural Geography, 11*(8), 865–881. doi:10.1080/14649365.2010.523841

Prentice, R. (1988). The Manx TT Races and residents' views: A case assessment of Doxey's 'Irridex'. *Scottish Geographical Magazine, 104*(3), 155–160. doi:10.1080/14702548808554774

Prentice, R. (1992). The Manx National Glens as treasured landscape. *Scottish Geographical Magazine, 108*(2), 119–127. doi:10.1080/00369229218736854

Ramshaw, G. (2010). Living heritage and the sports museum: Athletes, legacy and the Olympic hall of fame and museum, Canada Olympic Park. *Journal of Sport and Tourism, 15*(1), 45–70. doi:10.1080/14775081003770983

Ramshaw, G., & Gammon, S. (2010). On home ground? Twickenham Stadium tours and the construction of sport heritage. *Journal of Heritage Tourism, 5*(2), 87–102. doi:10.1080/17438730903484184

Ramshaw, G., & Hinch, T. (2006). Place identity and sport tourism: The case of the Heritage Classic. *Current Issues in Tourism, 9*(4–5), 399–418. doi:10.2167/cit270.0

Rose-Redwood, R., Alderman, D., & Azaryahu, M. (2010). Geographies of toponymic inscription: New directions in critical place-name studies. *Progress in Human Geography, 34*(4), 453–470. doi:10.1177/0309132509351042

Schofield, J. (2006). *Symmetry in heritage management practice.* Retrieved September 8, 2013, from http://humanitieslab.stanford.edu/23/1014

Smith, A. D. (1995). *Nations and nationalism in a global era.* Cambridge: Polity Press.

Smith, A. D. (2003). *Nationalism and Modernism. A critical survey of recent theories of nations and nationalism.* London: Taylor & Francis.

Smith, A. D. (2013). 'The land and its people': Reflections on artistic identification in an age of nations and nationalism. *Nations and Nationalism, 19*(1), 87–106. doi:10.1111/j.1469-8129.2012.00551.x

Smith, A., & Porter, D. (2004). Introduction. In A. Smith & D. Porter (Eds.), *Sport and national identity in the post-war world* (pp. 1–9). London: Routledge.

Thomson, R. L. (2000). The Manx language. In J. Belchem (Ed.), *A new history of the Isle of Man, Vol. 5, the modern period 1830–1999* (pp. 312–316). Liverpool: Liverpool University Press.

TT3D: Closer to the Edge. (2011). [Film] Directed by Richard De Aragues. Great Britain: Isle of Man Film/CinemaNX.

Turner, J. (2013). *Questions in Keys on upland tracks.* Retrieved September 12, 2013, from http://www.iomtoday.co.im/news/isle-of-man-news/questions-in-keys-on-upland-tracks-1-5485653

Vaukins, S. (2007). The Isle of Man TT Races: Politics, economics and national identity. *International Journal of Motorcycle Studies, 3*(3). Retrieved September 12, 2013, from http://ijms.nova.edu/November2007TT/IJMS_Artcl.Vaukins.html

Winterbottom, D. (2000). Economic history, 1830–1996'. In J. Belchem (Ed.), *A new history of the Isle of Man, Vol. 5, the modern period 1830–1999* (pp. 207–278). Liverpool: Liverpool University Press.

Woolridge, I. (2003, May 31). How many more will have to die? *Daily Mail Online*. Retrieved September 12, 2013, from http://www.dailymail.co.uk/debate/columnists/article-301493/How-die.html

Wright, D. (2007). *100 years of the Isle of Man TT: A century of motorcycle racing*. Marlborough: The Crowood Press.

Wright, R. K. (2012). Stadia, identity and belonging: Stirring the sleeping giants of sports tourism. In R. Shipway & A. Fyall (Eds.), *International sports events: Impacts, experiences and identities* (pp. 195–207). London: Routledge.

Heroes as heritage: the commoditization of sporting achievement

Sean J. Gammon

School of Sport, Tourism and the Outdoors, The University of Central Lancashire, Preston, UK

The paper aims to explore and develop discussion relating to sports heritage by introducing the proposition that sporting heroes can be equated to forms of both tangible and intangible heritage. It begins by identifying the nature and function of sports heroes, while delineating a basic sports hero typology based upon a dialectic process that drives the emotional responses of the spectator and/or fan. Furthermore, the paper explores the commoditization process of the sporting hero that reframes them into heritage "objects". These "objects" are, in turn, responsible for the intangible heritage achievements produced during their careers. It is argued that sports heroes represent a hitherto unexplored source of tourist interest (specifically related to authenticity and motivation) which may add to our understanding of heritage studies in general.

Introduction

Given that heritage is a fluid concept that is continually socially constructed it is little surprise that contemporary studies are increasingly focussing upon its interpretive and experiential qualities (Kim & Jamal, 2007; Park, 2014; Smith, 2006). Consequently, the idea of what heritage may or may not be has loosened somewhat, resulting in potentially new directions of research. Sport has been identified as being one such direction (Gammon & Ramshaw, 2007), though studies have predominantly focused upon recognising and protecting important sports sites, venues, and stadia (Beauchampe & Inglis, 2006; Inglis, 2004) rather than reflecting upon the less obvious manifestations of sports heritage. As a result there has been a notable lack of research and discussion that explores the more intangible features of sporting heritage as well as studies that further the debates of what might be generally considered as heritage.

Sports heroes are a fundamental element of the sporting landscape, and while being a popular topic in the sport history literature, has had scant coverage in works connected to heritage and tourism. Therefore, the primary aim of the paper is to discuss the actual and prospective linkages between sporting heroes and heritage. Moreover, the case will be made for living sporting heroes to be considered as a form of living heritage, and as a result to be recognised as attractions worthy of tourist experience and travel. Whilst the term "hero" generally refers to the great achievements and accomplishments of men, this is not the case in sport, and so when used in this paper we will refer to both sportsmen and sportswomen alike.

Sporting heroes

Debates surrounding the nature and purpose of heroes have attracted writers and commentators for millennia (Hughes-Hallett, 2004). The qualities of heroes are inherently difficult to pin down. From times of antiquity heroes have displayed often contradictory characteristics that, on the one hand, include feats of extraordinary greatness, sacrifice, and courage, while on the other, involve acts of selfishness, cruelty, and capriciousness. Some are revered as god-like – others as fragile, imperfect strugglers with feet of clay. Yet they are all noted as being exceptionally gifted in some ways, unique and powerfully inspirational whose maverick behaviour not only sets them apart from the rest but also ensures they stand alone. They can be law breakers as well as law makers, warriors, generals, politicians, philosophers, and many more. Modern sporting heroes are unsurprisingly a more recent feature upon the hero landscape; nevertheless, their inclusion and subsequent veneration spans more than two centuries (Barney, 1985; Crepeau, 1981; Holt, 1998; Hughson, 2009). It appears that sport needs heroes; that the many physical and mental challenges that sport often encompasses breeds individuals who are prepared to go beyond what is expected of them. Their deeds are rarely left unacknowledged by an adoring public who will defend and often elaborate a player's or athlete's achievements in a variety of fora. Accounts of their accomplishments can be found in the archives of clubs, libraries, museums, and halls of fame across the globe, yet the criteria that qualify them are opaque at best, and their purpose remains uncertain:

> ... a sport hero is like Hamlet without a Prince, and yet the varieties and purposes of sporting heroism are rarely examined. The sporting public is too busy worshipping to reflect on the objects of its fascination and those few whose business it is to take an analytical view have been absorbed in other things. (Holt & Mangan, 1996, p. 5)

It has been suggested that the choice and depiction of heroes is culturally framed, as heroism is always measured and (re) evaluated against the societal values of the day. This assertion has led many to observe that sporting hero-worship in North America differs to that practiced in Europe; the former based upon winning and winning well, the latter on aesthetics and Corinthian spirit (Holt & Mangan, 1996; Hughson, 2009; Rauch, 1996). Yet such distinctions fail to recognise the often transient nature of the hero; their adoration is not only dependent upon where they practise their trade – but also when. The stereotypical British portrayal of heroism, built upon understated great feats, tempered with humility and modesty have evolved into an appreciation for steadfastness, determination and triumph; characteristics more associated with American sporting culture. But heroes are hewn from many materials, some of which are undoubtedly more durable than others and some which display features that appeal to much wider audiences. The increasingly international nature of sport introduces and promotes new heroes; individuals whose triumphs are appreciated and assessed on a global scale.

There are more similarities than differences in how sporting heroes are chosen and defined, and when analysed collectively illustrate the various culturally driven nuisances and biases that contribute to our understanding of the term. For example, Barney (1985) sets out five very specific criteria: first, the hero must exhibit salient performance excellence – but such extraordinary abilities must be supported with the second criterion of moral excellence. They must behave with integrity and honesty both on and off the field of play. Heroes, according to Barney (1985), should also display strong altruistic tendencies, helping those less fortunate than themselves and/or inspiring others through support and unselfish deeds. The fourth criterion relates to the hero's ability to demonstrate theoretical and practical wisdom (Wann, Merrill, Russell, & Pease, 2001). Heroes should live in accordance to the values of the culture which they inhabit – practising financial propriety as well as general clean-living. The final criterion is that hero status cannot be bestowed on sportspeople during their lifetime. It is hoped that the passing of time will ensure that any potential damaging evidence relating to a given athlete be revealed before their "enshrine-ment". Barney's (1985) heroes are virtuous and almost saintly, whose initial notable sport-ing deeds are worth little if they are not supported by a wholesome and untarnished life outside the sport. Time, it is argued, will tease out any unfortunate tales concerning these "heroes in waiting", and so will add a sense of perspective and objectivity before hero status is accorded. However, time has a tendency to mythologise and venerate the greats to such an extent that perspective is lost; this is often the case in sport (Gammon, 2002; Gammon & Ramshaw, 2013; Redmond 1973). It is a truism that the further the passing of time, the more extraordinary the feats of heroism.

Hughson (2009) suggests, similar to Barney (1985), that their heroism can be con-sidered as emanating from one or both of their prowess and morality. Hughson (2009) does not propose that a hero is either one or the other, though in some cases there are players who failed to deliver the same level of achievement in their private lives as they did in their sporting careers. There is clearly a tension between their sporting endeavours and the personal conduct expected of those who have been given such exceptional skills. These moral judgements (both on and off the field of play) are undoubtedly culturally situ-ated and assessed, equating some behaviours (such as stretching the rules) being perceived by some as an artful display of overcoming authority, whilst others condemning them for blatant un-sportsman-like conduct. So, given such cultural diversity, is it possible to identify any salient characteristics which raise a sportsperson to heroic status? It appears that the literature tends to side-step the question, preferring to focus upon the function of heroes (discussed later in this paper) rather than nailing down specific features. As Bale (2006, p. 236) observes:

> The contestation of heroic qualities confirms the fractured nature of "heroism", a quality that is geographically and socially partial. Rarely is it asked *how* heroic one has to be in order to achieve the status of hero.

Nevertheless, it is worth exploring some common traits and features most often alluded to when describing heroes in order to distinguish them from the simply gifted and talented – of which there are numerous. Heroes are not just good at what they do, it is not, as Hughson (2009) points out, a simple process of identifying a career batting average or the number of wins a player or athlete accrued while competing, for it is as much to do with how such averages and successes were achieved, in what era, and under what conditions. For the deeds attained by the sporting hero, context is everything. In recent years there has been a steady dilution of the term hero, fuelled by a media that deals in hyperbole (Whannel, 1992) as well as a growing and ageing fan-base that nostalgically looks back upon a "golden age" of sport (Gammon & Ramshaw, 2013). Barney's (1985) contention that heroes can only be labelled as such after they have died sits uncomfortably with a public who are happy to pay premium prices to see and experience the sporting heroes of the day. There is room, it appears, for the coexistence of the mythologised heroes of the past and the emerging heroes of the present. Indeed, the most vehement debates in sport often involve the aesthetic and technical comparisons of previous heroes with those still competing or recently retired. Previous studies suggest that sporting heroes should of course demonstrate extraordinary technical prowess – but demonstrating great skill is not enough; for the hero should exude character, especially in the face of adversity (Holt & Mangan, 1996). Lines (2001) goes further, highlighting the very masculine qualities that we expect from heroes such as strength, bravery, competitiveness, and success, " ... all traditionally perceived to develop through sporting endeavours" (Lines, 2001, p. 289). But the elevation to hero status is not always based upon winning – as in some cases it is about losing with grace or failing courageously (Pivato, 1996; Rauch, 1996). Above all, however, the hero must have achieved something – usually something that was beyond what would normally be accepted as possible; a feat that in simple terms separates them from the rest. Their actions are rarely wasted on events where the outcome is unimportant or incidental, for, "it is in times of emergency that heroes are looked for and found" (Hughes-Hallett, 2004, p. 4). The above criteria outline some of the prominent qualities required to attain hero status, though they are largely dependent upon interpretation and illustration, equating to many discussions found in the literature supported by case studies and portraits (Bale, 2006; Crepeau, 1981; Holt & Mangan, 1996; Huntington-Whiteley, 1998; Hughson, 2009). There is little doubt that while specific cases help to put many of the discussions on heroism in context they also illustrate the very subjective nature of hero choice and depiction.

To what extent sporting heroes, or indeed any form of hero, serve a purpose that transcends their specific achievements is clearly a moot point. Hughes-Hallett (2004) contends that a country that has no need of heroes is indeed a fortunate one; that it is out of desperation that people feel a need to crave and worship a great champion or saviour. Others have taken a less cynical view, maintaining that heroes provide us with an ultimate ideal that can be both inspirational and life-affirming: "The hero shows us what we ought to be, and we make him a hero because we wish to be what he is. He calls us beyond ourselves, towards the ideal" (Crepeau, 1981, p. 24). So heroes are not sought so much out of desperation but out of necessity, and therefore can be perceived as an integral element of any culture (Hofstede, Hofstede, & Minkov, 2010). In many cases, as detailed earlier, the sports hero can be saddled with the *nom de plume* of role model for both adults and children alike (Biskup & Pfister, 1999; Lockwood & Kunda, 1997; Wann et al., 2001). This additional responsibility often pressurises both young and experienced sports people to promote morally acceptable lifestyles that can be at odds to the lives they genuinely lead. The extent and nature of such disparity, when exposed, can affect their hero status permanently (the revelations concerning Tiger Woods' private life may be a point in case). Additionally sporting heroes can act as potent instigators and symbols of nostalgia, offering what Wann et al. (2001) refer to as a compensatory function. Present day heroes and their deeds can reignite the great feats of yesteryear by encouraging the adoring fan of greatness past. Whereas retired heroes (if indeed heroes ever retire) act as living representations of a "superior" past that provides comfort and solace to those who hanker back to the days of their youth (Gammon & Ramshaw, 2013). Such nostalgic sentiment generates a further more pragmatic economic function (fuelled by an ever increasing older demographic) which uses heroes as emotive commodities. For example, the appearance of a sports hero can increase gate receipts, and inductions into halls of fame can positively impact upon both the organisation and the region in which it is based.

Heroes then are culturally formed and situated. The interpretation of courage, skill, achievement and any other related criteria is socially determined, as is the extent that such achievements are valued and nurtured. They represent a cultural ideal that people wish to protect, celebrate and ultimately emulate. Much like heritage, heroes, along with their valued deeds and achievements, are cherished and recorded for future generations to acknowledge and revere. The degree in which sporting heroes can be considered *bona fide* heritage is unclear and represents the main discussion in the next section.

The hero–heritage nexus

The idea that heritage can be alive is not new, but the suggestion that a living individual can be a tangible heritage object has had scant coverage in the literature. Living heritage is more commonly associated with the intangible elements linked to an existing community's rituals, craftwork, music, or language (Deacon, 2004). It has also been described as the live interpretation found in living history museums such as Beamish in the UK – or in the numerous re-enactment displays that aim in recreating important battles and conflicts from the past (Smith, 2006). From a sporting context Ramshaw's (2010) study introduces an additional perspective to how the living can be critical features of a museum's products. His case study on the Olympic Hall of Fame and Museum at Canada Olympic Park in Calgary explored how watching Olympic athletes train had not only become an integral part of the museum visit but also fulfilled a number of legacy initiatives. White (2013) offers a more specific interpretation of living sporting heritage, arguing that Cathy Freeman became not only a potent symbol of Australia's heritage (through her achievements at the 2000 Olympic Games), but moreover that she personified and embodied the heritage of her country:

> If we understand heritage as a process that constructs meaning about the past, then the construction of Cathy Freeman at the Sydney Games is illustrative of this process. It was, essentially, a visual construction of heritage based upon her body, her movements and the setting. (White, 2013, p. 166)

Freeman's sporting achievements (National, World and Olympic 400 metres Champion) certainly qualify her as a sporting hero, with her status galvanised through her success at the Sydney 2000 Games. Through her own ethnicity she became a powerful symbol for the struggles and injustices of indigenous Australians as well as a national hero of the predominant white population. She was the Australian poster girl for the 2000 Games which placed additional pressure and intense national expectation on her shoulders leading up to the 400 metres final. As discussed above, success is not in itself enough to elevate exceptional athletes to hero status – context is everything. Since Freeman's retirement in 2003 she has become involved in a number of charity initiatives and remains, for many, a national treasure (Stewart, 2013).

The term "national treasure" is often attributed to sporting heroes who have achieved a status that permeates beyond initial fan bases. However, to what extent that living sporting heroes can be perceived and/or interpreted as living tangible heritage is unclear. Categorisations of sporting heritage have been suggested, including the category of tangible moveable objects which broadly refers to the displays and artefacts transported for special sports exhibitions or museum relocation (Ramshaw & Gammon, 2007). Intuitively, it would seem logical to consider living sporting heroes as a prime example of tangible moveable objects, yet the term "objects" implies an inanimateness that is at odds with the very living human qualities of the players and athletes in question. A very different relationship exists between the quiescent features of valued sporting artefacts and the corporeal qualities of the living. For example, those who have an interest in heritage are often influenced and impressed by the patina of age in some traditional tangible objects such as buildings and pieces of art. Sports heroes age and change – we cannot stop that – though their inextricable physical decline can at times sadden us, while simultaneously reminding us of our own mortality. We cannot preserve or protect them in the same way we can of other inanimate objects, but we can preserve and celebrate their deeds and achievements. Halls of fame and sports museums undoubtedly attempt to identify and celebrate achievements deemed important enough to record and pass on to future generations (Snyder, 1991). Also, statues are being increasingly used to celebrate and acknowledge sporting greats, and are viewed as tangible symbols which help vitalise and cement fan identities (Stride, Wilson, & Thomas, 2013). The living hero is then a conduit to the past; one who embodies the extra-ordinary achievements and experiences that so many admire and look up to. They are pro-ducers of intangible and tangible heritage through both the recording and marking of their accomplishments as well as through the collection of related personal sporting paraphernalia. If indeed heroes are perceived as a form of living heritage, then their heritage moment is but a fleeting one. There is little their adoring public can do to preserve them or to sympath-etically restore them for the delectation of those who were not fortunate enough to witness their achievements first hand. We have to forgive their decline, as unlike conventional heri-tage objects the veneer of age inherent in the retired hero does not ennoble their status but can often detract and distract from their extraordinary achievements. And yet, they are still to be admired and gazed upon as authentic representations of the original that undeniably project, to many, the aura of the unique and irreplaceable (Benjamin, 1999). It is little wonder that the opportunity to see and listen to the greats has become big business (Fairley & Gammon, 2005; Gammon & Ramshaw, 2013). Evidently then, it would be mis-leading to suggest that the response to an ageing hero is always one of disappointment or regret. Many past heroes still compete, albeit at a lower level than in their prime; others have forged out new careers, accomplishing new goals – and by so doing have re-positioned themselves within the sporting lexicon.

Heritage commonly generates an emotional response from those that come in contact with it (Bagnall, 2003; Chen & Chen, 2010). Sporting heroes are no different. The nature of the interaction (direct or vicarious) between hero and spectator is a complex one, and is largely dependent upon the extent of respect and worship involved. Neverthe-less, the emotional response to the retired hero will be based upon an assessment between a hero's past and a hero's present. Therefore, a dialectic practice takes place whereby a spec-tator assesses and revisits the image(s) and achievements of a hero's past, with image(s) and events that have taken place since. As a consequence, hero assessment must be viewed as a process that potentially identifies a range of hero types; each of which share quite distinct relationships with sporting heritage. For example, some heroes go on to forge successful careers after they have retired from competition. This type of enriched heritage occurs when athletes' achievements, post retirement, add or eclipse those they accomplished as an athlete. Sebastian Coe's political career and subsequent leadership of the London 2012 Olympic Games or Franz Beckenbauer's football management and German ambassa-dorial triumphs may act as appropriate examples. But for many heroes, the often unremark-able and/or less visible careers chosen after their sporting successes mean that their heritage status is a faded one; where their past achievements remain the chief components of their heritage. But for some heroes the tension between the past and the present is more polem-ical, leading to what could be described as damaged heritage. This is likely to take place where there have been indiscretions since the hero's retirement, or when new misdemea-nours from their playing careers are retrospectively examined. The ex-England soccer player Paul Gascoigne whose extraordinary achievements on the field have been marred by his subsequent fight with alcoholism and wife-beating charges may act as an appropriate example, as would the major league baseball batter Pete Rose's gambling charges leading to his permanent ineligibility to the baseball hall of fame. Others have fared worse, where their injudiciousness has been so extreme as to potentially wipe out any of their career achievements – however heroic they may have been. In this case the heritage is more broken than damaged and can be best illustrated in the recent doping revelations associated with Lance Armstrong. Whether Armstrong will ever be able to be recognised as anything other than a cheat remains to be seen, though his story may well remain as part of the darker, less palatable features of sports heritage. Of course any assessment of the past with the present will, as intimated earlier, generate a number of varying interpretations and conclusions. Much like other forms of heritage (Dann & Seaton, 2001; Timothy & Boyd, 2006; Tunbridge & Ashworth, 1996), the interpretation of sporting heroism and moral character will vary depending upon specific cultural values and the extent of fan identification. For example, Diego Maradona's extraordinary and unquestionable abilities on the field have, for some, been tainted by his much publicised fight with drug and alcohol addiction. Moreover, the much debated "hand of god" incident during the 1986 World Cup generated a notable re-evaluation of Maradona's hero status. It must be noted that the incident took place with the back-drop of the Falklands war, culminating in Maradona's hero status being firmly secured in Argentina as the young rascal genius while being labelled in England as an exceptionally gifted cheat (Archetti, 1997). A less obvious example of contested sporting heritage can be explored through the record-making achievements of Roger Bannister (Bale, 2006). Bannister is credited with being the first runner to break the four minute barrier for running a mile – and in doing so achieved athletic immortality (Huntington-Whiteley, 1998). And yet his achievement at the time (1954) was considered, by some, to be overly scientific and inappropriately contrived; arguing that the record should have taken place in normal competitive conditions, rather than the meticulously planned pace-setting circumstances that occurred on the day. Such sentiments exemplify the predominant Corinthian spirit inherent in British Athletics at the time.

Of course, like all heritage, the extent that a hero is valued and cherished is very much dependent upon a number of cultural and personal indicators; least of which is the degree of fandom attached to the hero (Gammon, 2012; Wann et al., 2001). Therefore, in some cases a hero's incautions may well be forgiven by an adoring public who prefer to focus upon an individual's sporting career, rather than their more human frailties. Indeed, such practices may well stem from a need to shield fans' self-esteem and beliefs as opposed to any selfless strategy to protect the reputation of the hero in question. Occasionally, when associated with the anti-hero it is, paradoxically, the questionable moral qualities that are equally celebrated and vilified over and above a sports person's prowess. John McEnroe's infamous tirades on court and seeming disregard for authority may act as an appropriate example (Hughson, 2009). Nevertheless, irrespective of how heroes are perceived and labelled, there is a good deal of evidence that their often global notoriety has made them into heritage tourist attractions in their own right.

Tourism and the sporting hero – the commoditisation of sporting achievement

Cohen's (1988, p. 380) assertion that commodification takes place when, " ... things (and activities) come to be evaluated primarily in terms of their exchange value, in a context of trade, thereby becoming goods (and services) ... ", highlights the clinical and obvious economic nature of supply and demand in both sport and tourism domains. However, what the above definition accounts less for is the human objectification as commodity, along with the process whereby an object changes its commercial identity. The idea that human beings can be treated as commodities is not new (Appadurai, 1986) and, can, for example, be illustrated in the immoral practice of slavery (Kopytoff, 1986). But the idea that individuals can be perceived as heritage objects in their own right, and as a result generate tourism activity, has largely been neglected in the literature.

Linkages between sport and tourism are well founded (Gammon & Kurtzman, 2002; Hinch & Higham, 2011; Standeven & De Knop, 1998; Weed & Bull, 2009) and include studies that acknowledge the potential for the sporting past to ignite significant tourism receipts (Fairley & Gammon, 2005; Gammon & Ramshaw, 2007; Gibson, 1998; Ramshaw, Gammon, & Huang, 2013). More specifically there have been increased discussions that explore the heritage of sport and its impact upon the study of heritage in general (Phillips, 2012; Ramshaw & Gammon 2007). The most obvious instances where sporting heroes are directly used to attract visitors are through Masters' events and/or senior tours such as those popular in golf, tennis, and ice hockey (Ramshaw & Hinch, 2006). The draw to such events has been chiefly framed and explained around the nostalgia literature or the heritage components of the events themselves. While, the experience of seeing heroes once more may produce nostalgic emotions, there will undoubtedly be other experiences and motives at work; particularly in seeing, first-hand, genuine heroes in action. The events will still have a strong competitive element to them, though understandably the level of competition will fall below either the level they played at in their prime or the level performed by current players. The motive appears not to see how they were but to get closer to how they are now, "they do not hit the ball as hard and are clearly not as athletic as they used to be, but this seems not to distract from the 'authenticity' of the event" (Fairley & Gammon, 2005, p. 188).

To get even closer to sporting heroes, fantasy camps offer visitors the opportunity to directly interact with past heroes by creating camps whereby attendees will play and train alongside the sport stars of the past (Gammon, 2002). Camps will often incorporate sporting venues that are connected in some way to the team or player that determine its primary selling point, equating to the ultimate sporting experience:

> For the campers, regular guys for all walks of life, it's heaven. They share locker rooms with the retired stars, and meals and social time, gleaning in their knowledge and becoming raptured with their lore. (Schlossberg, 1996, p. 112)

The least studied demonstration of the commoditization of sport heroes are the increasingly popular special appearance events whereby sporting greats will (for, at times, a considerable fee) discuss their careers with a live audience. In some case, events will involve photo sessions with the sport hero as well fine dining and other related speakers. Wayne Gretzky (a Canadian ice hockey icon) uses these types of appearances to raise funds for his own charity-based foundation and in doing so reinforces his already extraordinary hero status. Depending on the notoriety of the hero, tickets can demand high prices and will be affected by the chance or promise of some forms of interaction with the hero. For example, "an evening with" Wayne Gretzky can cost around $1999.00 (CDN) (Frameworth Sports Marketing, 2013). Additionally, heroes can be used to enrich and support other products and services. Stadium tours are now an accepted offering for the majority of major sporting venues and will range in their complexity and popularity (Ramshaw et al., 2013). For a premium price many tours (e.g. Emirates stadium: Arsenal FC) will include an ex star of the club to show patrons around – sharing anecdotes and signing photographs, etc.

As intimated above authenticity is an important element of the visitors experience at such events. To take a dualistic perspective, there is an authenticity to the bodies the heroes inhabit and so they offer insights that are unlikely to be divorced from reality. The demand for visitors, to see them in the flesh, indicates their importance to not just the sporting landscape but to the broader cultural fabric too. This may indicate that the sports hero has become no different from other notable celebrities; that it is their simple notoriety that perpetuates the public's curiosity towards them. For example, Turner (2014) believes that "the desire for the authentic – to reach the core of the personality, to find out what 'they are really like' – is as fundamental to the sports fans as to the film fan" (p. 24). It is beyond the scope of this paper to explore the definitional vagaries and complexities of the term celebrity, as this has been discussed in some detail elsewhere (Monaco, 1976; Rojek, 2001, 2012; Turner, 2014). Nevertheless, it is worth pointing out that there appears no clear consensus as to whether sports heroes are in some way separate from celebrity (Boorstin, 1971; Shuart, 2007) or, as Rojek (2001) and Drucker (1997) argue, are in fact one in the same thing. There is undoubtedly a case to be made that sporting heroes have become part of the celebrity culture inherent in many developed societies, yet this demeans their standing and durability. There is a shadow of ephemerality and superficiality that runs through the term celebrity, indicated by its likely Latin route of *celere* – meaning swift. It may be the case that their time in the spot-light is fleeting but their deeds and accomplishments can live on for generations. There is a good deal of evidence that fans and followers will pursue their heroes and pay a premium price to get close to them, yet their motives and experiences require further investigation by both sport and tourism scholars alike.

Conclusion

The extent in which sporting heroes can be interpreted as tangible manifestations of living heritage is unclear but the case that their achievements be considered as intangible heritage is less contentious. Our rejection of living heroes being considered as heritage objects undoubtedly stems from their obvious finite qualities. From an anatomical viewpoint they are not much different from those who worship them; for it is what their bodies have achieved and experienced that separates them from the ordinary. In this sense they are no different than the more conventional structures we bestow the status of heritage to. If indeed we are to accept that heritage is in the eye of the beholder and that nothing truly has inherent heritage qualities then the case for living heroes may be more confidently made. Sporting heroes personify the limitless boundaries of sporting achievement and so remind those less able of what can be realised in their own lives. Yet, in some cases the hero struggles to carve out new life directions – and to set out new goals. They carry around with them the often heavy weight of their own sporting achievements, which in turn prevents them from making a successful life away from the gaze of the fan. Others will use their sporting achievements as a vehicle to new career paths and successes, and in doing so, reposition their hero status. But whatever their heritage status, whether enriched, faded, damaged, contested – or even broken, there will always be an audience prepared to experience them in the flesh one last time. There is little doubt that demand to see and get close to them makes heroes a much desired commodity, and establishes many of them as an integral part of sports heritage and beyond.

References

Appadurai, A. (Ed.). (1986). *The social life of things. Commodities in cultural perspective.* Cambridge: Cambridge University Press.

Archetti, E. P. (1997). And give joy to my heart. Ideology and emotions in the Argentinian cult of Maradona. In G. Armstrong & R. Guilianotti (Eds.), *Entering the field. New perspectives on world football* (pp. 3–52). Oxford: Berg.

Bagnall, G. (2003). Performance and performativity at heritage sites. *Museum and Society, 1*(2), 87–103.

Bale, J. (2006). How much of a Hero? The fractured image of Roger Bannister. *Sport in History, 26*(2), 235–247.

Barney, R. K. (1985). The hailed, the haloed, and the hallowed: Sport heroes and their qualities – An analysis and hypothetical model for their commemoration. In Müller, N. Rühl, J. K. (Eds.), *Olympic scientific congress sport history.* July 19–26, 1984 (pp. 88–103). Niedernhausen: University of Oregon, Eugene/Oregon, Official Report.

Beauchampe, S., & Inglis, S. (2006). *Played in Birmingham. Charting the heritage of a city at play.* Birmingham: English Heritage.

Benjamin, W. (1999). *Illuminations* (H. Arendt, Trans.). London: Pimlico.

Biskup, C., & Pfister, G. (1999). I would like to like her/him: Are athletes role-models for boys and girls? *European Physical Education Review, 5*(3), 199–218.

Boorstin, D. (1971). *The image: A guide to pseudo-events in America.* New York: Atheneum.

Chen, C. F., & Chen, F. S. (2010). Experience quality, perceived value, satisfaction and behavioural intentions for heritage tourists. *Tourism Management, 31,* 29–35.

Cohen, E. (1988). Authenticity and commoditization in tourism. *Annals of Tourism Research, 15*(3), 371–386.

Crepeau, R. (1981). Sport heroes and myth. *Journal of Sport and Social Issues, 5*(23), 23–31.

Dann, G. M. S., & Seaton, A. V. (2001). Slavery, contested heritage and thanatourism. *International Journal of Hospitality & Tourism Administration, 2*(3/4), 1–29.

Deacon, H. (2004). Intangible heritage in conservation management planning: The case of Robben Island. *International Journal of Heritage Studies, 10*(3), 309–319.

Drucker, S. (1997). The mediated sports hero. In S. Drucker & R. Cathart (Eds.), *The mediated sports hero. American heroes in middle age* (pp. 82–96). Creskill, NJ: Hampton.

Fairley, S. and Gammon, S. (2005). Something lived, something learned: Nostalgia's expanding role in sport tourism. *Sport in society: Cultures, commerce, Media, Politics, 8*(2), 182–197.

Frameworth Sports Marketing. (2013). *A very special evening with Wayne Gretzky.* Retrieved from http://frameworth.com/cart/skin1/images/Gretzky.pdf

Gammon, S. (2002). Fantasy, nostalgia and the pursuit of what never was. In S. Gammon & J. Kurtzman (Eds.), *Sport tourism: Principles and practice* (pp. 61–71). Eastbourne: LSA Publications.

Gammon, S. (2012). Sports events: Typologies, people and place. In S. J. Page & J. Connell (Eds.), *The Routledge handbook of events* (pp. 104–118). London: Routledge.

Gammon, S., & Kurtzman, J. (Eds). (2002). *Sport tourism: Principles and practice.* Eastbourne: LSA Publications.

Gammon, S., & Ramshaw, G. (2007). *Heritage, sport and tourism: Sporting pasts – Tourist futures.* London: Routlege.

Gammon, S., & Ramshaw, G. (2013). Nostalgia and sport. In A. Fyall & B. Garrod (Eds.), *Contemporary cases in sport* (pp. 201–219). London: Goodfellow.

Gibson, H. (1998). Sport tourism: A critical analysis of research. *Sport Management Review, 1*(1), 45–76.

Hinch, T., & Higham, J. (2011). *Sport tourism development.* Clevedon: Channel View.

Hofstede, G. H., Hofstede, G. J., & Minkov, M. (2010). *Cultures and organizations: Software of the mind: International cooperation and its importance for survival.* London: McGraw-Hill.

Holt, R. (1998). Champions, heroes and celebrities: Sporting greatness and the British public. In J. Huntington-Whiteley (Ed.), *The Book of British sporting heroes* (pp. 12–25). London: National Portrait Gallery.

Holt, R., & Mangan, J. A. (1996). Prologue: Heroes of a European past. In R. Holt & J. A. Mangan (Eds.), *European heroes. Myth, identity, sport.* London: Frank Cass.

Hughes-Hallett, L. (2004). *Heroes. A history of hero worship.* New York: Anchor Books.

Hughson, J. (2009). On sporting heroes. *Sport in Society: Cultures, Media, Media, Politics, 12*(1), 85–101.

Huntington-Whiteley, J. (1998). *The Book of British sporting heroes.* London: National Portrait Gallery.

Inglis, S. (2004). *Played in Manchester. The architectural heritage of city at play.* London: English Heritage.

Kim, H. and Jamal, T. (2007). Tourist quest for existential authenticity. *Annals of Tourism Research, 34*(1), 181–201.

Kopytoff, I. (1986). The cultural biography of things: Commoditization as process. In A. Appadurai (Ed.), *The social life of things. Commodities in cultural perspective* (pp. 64–94). Cambridge: Cambridge University Press.

Lines, G. (2001). Villains, fools or heroes? Sports stars as role models for young people. *Leisure Studies, 24*(4), 285–303.

Lockwood, P., & Kunda, Z. (1997). Superstars and ME: Predicting the impact of role models on the self. *Journal of Personality and Social Psychology, 73*(1), 91–103.

Monaco, J. (Ed.). (1976). *Celebrity. The media as image makers*. New York: Delta.

Park, H. Y. (2014). *Heritage tourism*. London: Routledge.

Phillips, M. G. (Ed.). (2012). *Representing the sporting past in museums and halls of fame*. London: Routledge.

Pivato, S. (1996). Italian cycling and the creation of a catholic hero: The Bartali myth. In R. Holt, J. A. Mangan, & P. Lanfranchi (Eds.), *European heroes. Myth, identity, sport* (pp. 128–138). London: Frank Cass.

Ramshaw, G. (2010). Living heritage and the sports museum: Athletes, legacy and the Olympic hall of fame and museum, Canada Olympic park. *Journal of Sport and Tourism, 15*(1), 45–70.

Ramshaw, G., & Gammon, S. (2007). More than just nostalgia? Exploring the heritage sport tourism nexus. In S. Gammon & G. Ramshaw (Eds.), *Heritage, sport and tourism: Sporting pasts – tourist futures* (pp. 9–21). London: Routledge.

Ramshaw, G., Gammon, S., & Huang, W. (2013). Acquired pasts and the commodification of borrowed heritage: The case of the bank of America stadium tour. *Journal of Sport and Tourism, 18*(1), 17–31.

Ramshaw, G., & Hinch, T. (2006). Place identity and sport tourism: The case of the heritage ice hockey event. *Current Issues in Tourism, 5*(4–5), 399–418.

Rauch, A. (1996). Courage against cupidity: Carpentier and dempsey – symbols of cultural confrontation. In R. Holt, J. A. Mangan, & P. Lanfranchi (Eds.), *European heroes. Myth, identity, sport* (pp. 156–168). London: Frank Cass.

Redmond, G. (1973). A plethora of shrines: Sport in the museum and the hall of fame. *Quest, 19*, 41–48.

Rojek, C. (2001). *Celebrity*. London: Routledge.

Rojek, C. (2012). *Fame attack: The inflation of celebrity and its consequences*. London: Bloomsbury.

Schlossberg, H. (1996). *Sports marketing*. Oxford: Blackwell Business.

Shuart, J. (2007). Heroes in sport: Assessing celebrity endorser effectiveness. *International Journal of Sports Marketing & Sponsorship, 1*, 124–140.

Smith, L. (2006). *Uses of heritage*. London: Routledge.

Snyder, E. (1991). Sociology of nostalgia: Halls of fame and museums in America. *Sociology of Sport Journal, 8*, 228–38.

Standeven, J., & De Knop, P. (1998). *Sport tourism*. Leeds: Human Kinetics.

Stewart, C. (2013). 2000: Cathy Freeman, olympic champion. *The Weekend Australian Magazine*. Retrieved from http://www.theaustralian.com.au/news/features/cathy-freeman-olympic-champion/story-e6frg8h6-1226723751642

Stride, C., Wilson, J. P., & Thomas, F. (2013). Honouring heroes by branding in bronze: Theorizing the UK's football statuary. *Sport in Society, 16*(6), 749–771.

Timothy, D. J., & Boyd, S. W. (2006). Heritage tourism in the 21st Century: Valued traditions and new perspectives. *Journal of Heritage Tourism, 1*(1), 1–16.

Tunbridge, J., & Ashworth, G. (1996). *Dissonant heritage: The management of the past as a resource in conflict*. Chichester: Wiley.

Turner, G. (2014). *Understanding celebrity*. London: Routledge.

Wann, D., Merrill, M., Russell, G., & Pease, D. (2001). *Sports fans: The psychology and social impacts of spectators*. New York: Routledge.

Weed, M., & Bull, C. (2009). *Sports tourism: Participants, policy and providers*. London: Butterworth-Heinemann.

Whannel, G. (1992). *Fields in vision: Television, sport and cultural transformation*. London: Routledge.

White, L. (2013). Cathy Freeman and Australia's indigenous heritage: A new beginning for an old nation at the Sydney 2000 Olympic Games. *International Journal of Heritage Studies, 19*(2), 153–170.

A Canterbury tale: imaginative genealogies and existential heritage tourism at the St. Lawrence Ground

Gregory Ramshaw

Department of Parks, Recreation and Tourism Management, Clemson University, Clemson, SC, USA

At its most innate, heritage is biological, and perceptions of our own origins can drive many heritage journeys. However, like many heritage excursions, genealogical travel can also fuse objective fact with imagination in the search for meaning and identity. This paper explores a genealogical journey to a cricket ground in Kent, where the search for a family member's past seamlessly merged with broader heritage constructions. Through this journey, it was found that heritage could be seen as a series of dualities; a mixture of collective and individual, objective and imaginative, and tangible and existential. Furthermore, it considers that heritage sport tourism – a topic broadly concerned with extrinsic, tangible heritage such as sports sites, sports museums, and sporting artifacts, can also be viewed through a more existential lens.

Introduction

The role of heritage in tourist journeys has received considerable attention in recent years, in part because of the immense social, cultural, and economic role heritage tourism plays in both the lives of tourists and the communities and sites they visit. Because the term "heritage" is so ubiquitous, and because it has been applied across the board to many different activities, items, and sites, heritage and tourism scholars have had to come to grips with what heritage "is" (as opposed to, say, history, memory, nostalgia, and other forms of cultural representation). According to Timothy (2011), there is widespread acceptance that heritage is the present use of the past – in other words, how we use the past as a resource today, be it for selling antiques, promoting tourist sites, or even making political or identity claims. As such, heritage can be, according to Lowenthal (1998), an "act of faith" – believing in a past suited to our present-day needs rather than as a critical understanding of the past in its own context. Similarly, heritage tourism is typically involved in the experiential aspects of visiting sites either from a distant past or that were witness to famous past events – be they historical houses, castles, cathedrals, battlefields, and the like (Timothy & Boyd, 2006).

However, there has been some debate as to the core of heritage tourism. While it seems logical that heritage tourism should and must include codified and institutionalized sites that are recognized, enshrined, conserved, and promoted, heritage is dynamic and can be applied to most anything, anywhere, at any time which, logically, would also apply to many different types of locations as well. Poria, Butler, and Airey (2001, 2003) posit that understanding where heritage tourism occurs should not be strictly relative to the historic merits of a location, but rather must also consider the dynamic between tourist motivation and tourist perception of one's own heritage. At its most innate, heritage is biological, and perceptions of our own origins can drive many heritage journeys to locations not normally considered to be part of heritage tourism itineraries. According to Lowenthal (1998), "blood is still widely held to determine not only pigment and physique but character and fate" (p. 202). As such, even our bloodlines are contextual. Heritage is not a finite resource, according to Ashworth (2008) – we create it as we need it. We may trumpet the famous or the infamous aspects of our biological pasts, while ignoring or marginalizing that which does not fuel our search for identity, or for ourselves. Like any other heritage, therefore, an existential heritage tourist journey is subject to the same limitations as other heritage: it edits, marginalizes, brags, and ignores as required. But the search for ourselves, at the sites and locations where we believe we are both genetically bound and feel have determined something of our destiny, may be the most basic yet powerful form of heritage tourism.

What follows, then, is a story of one such existential heritage journey. Existentialism is frequently a part of tourism, where tourists attempt to locate something of a "true" identity without being bound by the constraints of "real life" and its day-to-day routines (Brown, 2013; Wang, 1999). Similarly, self-reflexivity – particularly, the incorporation of autobiographical narratives – often intersects with heritage tourism (Chronis, 2012; Rickly-Boyd, 2009; Timothy, 2008). This journey was existential, in so far as it seemed to be more than mere curiosity and rather intersected with a deep sense of identity, both in terms of roots and fate. It was also self-reflexive, as impressions of my own heritage and sense of identity were read – and, indeed, had to be read – into the experience for it to make sense to me. However, this journey was not, in a traditional sense, a search for genealogical truth but, rather, was part fact and part faith, as is much of heritage tourism. Unlike many heritage expeditions that involve the search for roots, this trip did not include a family house, an old cemetery, or a local archive. Rather, the focus of this journey was at sports venue, specifically at the St. Lawrence Ground in Canterbury at second division four-day match between Kent and Leicestershire in May 2012. Though this journey was, in part, a search for the spirit of my Grandfather – a man who loved cricket, spent much of his leisure time at various cricket pitches in Kent, including at the St. Lawrence Ground, and to whom I feel strongly, even cosmically, connected – and was centrally about understanding him through a location that seemed to be important in his life, it also ended up revealing something to me about the more collective manifestations of England's sport and leisure culture. What I hope this exploration reveals is not only that heritage tourism can occur most anywhere – even at a sports venue – but also that heritage tourism can exist at many different levels and have multiple meanings, often simultaneously. Heritage exists on many scales, from the global to the personal (Graham, Ashworth, & Tunbridge, 2000; Timothy & Boyd, 2003), although personal heritages tend to be overlooked in heritage tourism. As Timothy (1997) reminds us, "personal heritage attractions draw people who possess emotional connections to a particular place" (p. 753). Considering Leiper's (1990) attraction system, a personal heritage "marker" that connects the tourist to the location could be almost anything – from an old photograph to a story from a parent or grandparent – and, as such, the number of personal heritage attractions is considerable and could, therefore, include sports venues. What I hope this exploration shows is not only that heritage tourism can occur most anywhere – even at a sports venue – but also that heritage tourism can exist at many different levels and have multiple meanings, often simultaneously. Furthermore, what this experience reveals is, perhaps, that heritage tourism as a series of dualities – fusing the collective with the individual, the objective and tangible with the speculative, imaginative, and existential – all the while constructing a very real and very powerful form of authenticity.

Imagining my grandfather

By all indications, my grandfather – Richard "Dick" Cosh – was the quintessential post-war Englishman, except for the fact that he was not actually born in England. Though he was Canadian by birth – and that he only spent part of his life in England – his activities and interests were almost entirely centered on English culture. He was well read in the classics of English literature, knew (and could recite) English poetry and song, and was a fervent follower of English politics. He was a schoolteacher – a profession that took him throughout Canada and across the Atlantic and back – but wherever he and his family went, his heart always seemed to remain in England and, more specifically, in Kent. Perhaps, it is unsurprising then, as I spoke with my mother about her father, that his greatest passion, and his strongest link to English culture, was cricket. Not content to be a spectator or mere follower, he was an umpire for many years and, upon his untimely death in 1963, was chair of the Edmonton (Canada) Cricket Club. His family – my grandmother, mother, my aunt, and my uncle – would spend most every summer weekend at the local cricket club, watching my grandfather umpire but, probably, enjoying the all-too-short Canadian summers. In speaking with my mother, those weekends watching cricket were some of the happiest of her childhood.

A few years back, my mother unearthed some old photographs of her father. Though she found dozens of pictures, the vast majority of them were of my grandfather in his white umpire's coat posing with players at various cricket grounds around Kent (Figure 1). While I found these very interesting, one batch of photographs in particular piqued my interest. They appeared to be all from a family vacation through Kent in August 1953, just before the family moved to Canada. There were pictures of the picnics and sandcastles by the seaside and a family photo in front of Canterbury Cathedral. However, there were multitudes of photographs of one particular match and ground. Most of the cricket photos had autographs on the back and, after a bit of online sleuthing, turned up that most of them were from an August 1953 three-day match between Kent and Australia at the St. Lawrence Ground in Canterbury (for the record, Australia won by an innings and 176 runs) (Cricket Archive, 2012).

The photos showed players from both sides walking on to the pitch from the pavilion (Figure 2), various angles and shots of the ground, and a series of team photographs with both the Kent and Australian teams intermingled (Figure 3). Given that the photos had autographs from both teams, I assume that my grandfather took the photos on the opening day and managed to have the film developed in time to have them autographed by the end of the match. Seemingly, he also appeared to be very fond of the ground, though whether he had umpired there or had seen matches there before I do not know. In any event, it appears that going to that ground for that match was extremely important to my grandfather and, given that it was near the end of his time in England, may have been one of the last experiences he would have had in the country.

Figure 1.   Richard "Dick" Cosh my grandfather, far right. Family members said that this was from his umpiring days in Kent in the early 1950s, though it is unknown at which ground this picture was taken. (Photo from Gregory Ramshaw)

Searching for the authentic in heritage journeys

Discussions of authenticity are, perhaps, one of the most well-worn paths in both tourism and heritage. Our search for some sort of objective or contextual reality in both our heritage and our tourism can be of paramount importance to our connection, understanding, and enjoyment of cultural heritage tourism, although what makes something authentic is often highly contested (Chhabra, Healey, & Sills, 2003; Cohen, 1988; MacCannell, 1973). In recent years, the debate has shifted from authenticity of the toured object, toward an understanding of the authenticity of the experience (Bruner, 2005; Rickly-Boyd, 2012). Ashworth (2008) perhaps states it most bluntly, arguing that:

> Authenticity (in heritage tourism) relates not to the object or physical site but only to the experience. Any other definition of authenticity is at best a delusion and at worst a professional conspiracy. Only the user can define the authenticity of a heritage experience. (p. 25)

Ashworth claims that a modern reconstruction of a historic site, for example, provides a more authentic experience than touring the original remnants of the site. Certainly, being in contact or proximity of an objectively verified authentic artifact can be a powerful experience. However, what Ashworth's argument highlights is the role of perception in tourist journeys. Wang's (1999) discussion of existential authenticity highlights the relationship of our sense of self, and our relationship with others, in the construction of tourist journeys as authentic. Indeed, perhaps if we believe or feel that a tourist experience is connected to us

Figure 2. Members of the touring Australian team at the St. Lawrence Ground in Canterbury, August 1953. Cricketers are identified at Arthur Morris (left) and Lindsay Hassett (right). (Photo from Gregory Ramshaw)

or our personal perceptions of our own heritage, then perhaps it becomes an authentic experience. Of course, there can be interplay between both external and internal constructions of authenticity. The artifact may indeed be objectively authentic – and the tourist may *believe* that the artifact is authentic, making it a powerful experience. Even constructed aspects of authentic cultural display, at a religious service or a sporting match for example, are often not pseudo-events, conscious of the tourist gaze. Rather, for the tourist, they can be both externally authentic displays of culture while also being part of the tourist's perception of his or her own culture, heritage, and identity (such as sharing the same faith or fandom).

"You are a lot like him"

I never knew my grandfather but, serendipitously, I have traveled a similar path. Like him, I was born in Canada and I am employed in education. We even have an eerily similar appearance. We also shared fondness for England after spending much of our adult lives there. Like him, I also acquired an interest and taste for various English pastimes, most recently teaching myself to understand (or at least follow) cricket. I did not do this, initially at least, as a way of connecting with my family's past. In fact, I was rather unaware of my grandfather's cricket history. Rather, taking MacGregor's (2006) view that "it is impossible to know a people until you know the game they play" (p. ix), cricket represented for me the epitome of English cultural identity – and, if I were to somehow understand England (or, at least a version thereof), I ought to know something of this sport. It was hardly a chore. I read

Figure 3.   Australian and Kent teams, St. Lawrence Ground, August 1953. (Photo from Gregory Ramshaw)

books – both technical and poetic – about the sport, watched an ever-increasing number of matches on-line or on television, and toured Lord's twice in a three-year span. It was such a beautiful sport, played in beautiful places – I fell in love with it, or at least the bucolic version of it I had created in my imagination. It was only after my mother unearthed those photographs of her father, and talked about his abiding interest in cricket, that it became more than just a sport. "You are a lot like him", she said, "you love books, you adore England, and you've even acquired an interest in his favourite pastime". She talked about how the sport connected him to England, and continued to connect him when he moved back to Canada. And, in a sense, I suppose cricket connected me to him, or at least made me want to know more about him. I often imagined what it would have been like had we met and had he been there while I was growing up. Would I have been influenced to take up cricket rather than ice hockey? Would I have spent summer days at the local ground, watching him umpire and learning the nuances of bowling, batting, and the turn of a wicket? Would we have ever returned to his beloved Kent, and would he have showed me his favorite grounds and told me stories of famous players and matches? In a sense, cricket helped me create a counterfactual personal narrative, a parallel universe where I knew my grandfather and he knew me. Not all of my imagined conversations with him were about cricket. But, it was through cricket that I got to know him.

Personal sport heritage journeys

Tourism studies have become ever-more fractured and subdivided, in part because our journeys are interpreted to be ever-more individualistic. As such, many subsections of tourism are adjective-prefaced – including, of course, heritage tourism. At times, these subdivisions can share commonalities and are combined, as is the case examining sport-based heritage journeys or, as Ramshaw and Gammon (2005) term it, heritage sport tourism, where elements of heritage and sport are part of the touristic landscape. Heritage sport tourism reflects much of the thinking of both heritage and sport tourism studies, in that the attraction is external to us. In other words, the "sport heritage" resides at a hall of fame or sports museum, at a famous sporting venue, or in the witnessing of a sporting tradition or ritual. Indeed, part of the appeal of heritage sport tourism is walking in the footsteps of famous sportspeople, or seeing where infamous sporting events or moments took place (Gammon & Fear, 2007; Ramshaw & Gammon, 2010). The idea that sport heritage could also involve personal heritage, or that sport could be the vehicle for journeys of self-discovery, has yet to be fully understood. Indeed, some sport heritage experiences – such as the sport fantasy camp, where patrons connect with both their own memories or through the nostalgia of one's own former, athletic self – could be considered a type of personal sport heritage journey (Gammon, 2002). However, most sport heritage still deals with more collective, broader forms of heritage. We can walk in the footsteps of legends – but normally only if that legend is a famous athlete whom everyone knows and admires. Rarely is sport heritage understood not through infamy but through blood.

Walking in his footsteps

Bale (2003) argues that psychologically we associate particular sports with particular regions, even going so far as to construct prototypical landscapes for these sports; images of what the sports look like (or, rather, ought to look like) in these regions. Calling these "imaginative geographies of sport", Bale (2003, p. 168) also quotes at length a passage from Macdonnell (1935), describing a rustic image of cricket in Kent, the "Garden of England". The quote, far too lengthy to be repeated here, nevertheless speaks of a bucolic rural England, "unspoilt by factories and financiers and tourists and hustle" dotted by red-roofed cottages, rickety gates, and church spires, where the only sounds are the "bees lazily drift(ing)" and where one can see "white butterflies flopp(ing) their aimless way among the gardens". Then, Macdonnell describes the cricket field – a "mass of daisies and buttercups and dandelions, tall grasses and thisledown, and great clumps of dark red sorrel, except, of course, of the oblong patch in the centre – mown, rolled, watered – a smooth, shining emerald of grass … the Wicket".

Having grown up in Western Canada, and having played ice hockey most of my life, I was familiar with the romantic tropes of sporting landscapes. The sport of my childhood shares much in common with cricket, as the ponds of Canadian winters are mythical, egalitarian places where boys of all ages and abilities can pretend to become hockey legends (Ramshaw & Hinch, 2006). Thus, as I walked through the city center of Canterbury en route to the St. Lawrence Ground, I knew not to expect exactly the chocolate box representation of cricket, but still wanted to see an echo of the sport and the field that appears to define a country, not to mention that it meant so much to my grandfather's identity. Of course, walking through the medieval city did make me think about what my grandfather would, and would not, have recognized in Canterbury. Certainly, many of the shops had changed – I doubt there were many tattoo parlors or Thai restaurants in his day – but, some aspects would have certainly seemed familiar. Adding to this was the fact that my journey just preceded the Diamond Jubilee celebrations and, like many cities throughout the country, Canterbury's shops and storefronts were gearing up for the festivities. I was reminded that his trip to Canterbury would have taken place some weeks after the

Coronation in 1953, and I would expect that there may have been a similar feeling of national celebration throughout that summer. The papers during my visit certainly discussed how the bunting, flags, and general feeling of patriotism leading up to the Jubilee was a throwback to the 1950s, so the serendipity of sharing a similar shared national cultural experience as my grandfather did only added to the experience.

Arriving at the St. Lawrence Ground at around half-past 10 on the first day of a (scheduled) 4-day match between Kent and Leicestershire, I was immediately taken as to how similar the ground was to the vision I had constructed in my mind. Like the city center, there were differences at the ground that would have immediately been recognizable to my grandfather (such as the advertising and digital scoreboard), but, otherwise, this would have been a place that he knew. Of course, there were not red-roofed cottages, church spires and such – nor, of course, would there have been in my grandfather's day – but, though this was a ground near a busy city center, I was amazed at how much it felt like a different space than the surrounding community. It was a warm, humid, and somewhat hazy day, but one could hear the breeze blowing, the birds chirping, and the gentle conversation between spectators in the minutes before the start of play. It was as perfect a representation of English cricket as I could have hoped (Figure 4).

Being new to the sport and still unfamiliar with its nuances, an English colleague was kind enough to join me for the match, patiently explaining the ebbs and flows of each day's play – the fielding, the bowling, and the meanings of different applause (encouragement for a bowler, an ovation at a good at bat, mocking contempt for a poorly played shot, and so on). He also helped me to translate some of the cultural aspects of the spectators –

Figure 4. Kent vs. Leicestershire at the St. Lawrence Ground, Canterbury, May 2012. (Photo by Gregory Ramshaw)

through accents, choice of reading material, and topics of conversation (mostly well-off, and likely conservative). Being that the match began on a Wednesday, I did not expect that there would be many families or even working-aged people at the ground. However, I was taken back at how the demographic was entirely white, many who seemed retired (or of retiring age), and male – many of whom were by themselves. Perhaps in retrospect, it was rather appropriate that this sporting séance of sorts was to have a more fraternal feel to it. The ground was by no means full, though it appeared to be a good-sized crowd given the mid-week start. I was somewhat prepared to be one of the few in attendance, given that I had read much about the demise of long-form cricket in general (Thompson, 2012) and county cricket in particular (ESPN CricInfo, 2012); however, it seemed that there were a fair number of spectators. Talking with a few of the club personnel, as well as overhearing some of the conversations between regulars, the large-ish crowd was due, in large part, to the excellent weather. The Club had been hard pressed to attract many people through the first six weeks of their season because of poor weather (Pearson, 2012), but it seemed that there were more people there than the proverbial "two old-men and a dog".

I was fully prepared to stay the fully 4 days if necessary, attempting to tune my North American sporting palate, raised on 2 hours and 20 minutes events, complete with exploding scoreboards and buxom cheerleaders, to something slow, quiet, and rather archaic. When I tell my American colleagues that I have acquired a taste for cricket, the immediate response is usually thus: (a) cricket makes no sense at all and (b) even if you could follow it, how (or why) would you watch something that lasts four days? My response is typically, (a) it is actually an easier sport to follow than baseball and (b) a four-day match is no different than a four-day golf tournament. Of course, I had never watched from tip-to-toe a golf tournament, nor had I actually watched a full first-class match. Yes, I had followed on-line and listened to Test Match Special following a day's play, but I do not think I was fully prepared for the spectating endurance of a four-day match. Cultural spectacle and genealogical searches were all fine and good, but they are no fun at all if they become tedious.

Much to my delight, however, I found the experience to be ideal. Far from being bored, I was swept up in the beauty of the match: the time and the pace, the ebb and flow of the game, the birds chirping and the wind blowing through the trees, the conversations, the pints, and sandwiches at lunch, the second pint at tea – all of it. As I was taking in the match, I was reminded of Thompson's (2012) essay about his experiences watching test cricket for the first time. He was sent from the USA to watch England vs. India at Lord's in 2011 and, like me, he felt slightly uneasy at the prospect of watching a full test match. However, by the final day, he found that

> I'm into the rhythm. I enjoy the silence. I work a crossword puzzle, looking up every minute or so to see the bowler begin his run. A thought assembles in the white spaces. Being here feels like a vacation, not just because the days are free of responsibility, but because they feel so different from the rest of my life. The world is full of people trying to slow down. There's a slow food movement, and rejection of consumerism and industrial convenience. Knitting, baking, urban farming. There's yoga ... People are seeking something. Maybe test cricket is part of that search. (N.P.)

Despite this being a new and entirely original revelation to me, I suspect this was simply an understood truth by the men watching the match. My English associate mentioned, during one of our many conversations over the course of the contest, that one of his colleagues had done some research about what people do during seaside vacations. Of course, people listed a variety of activities, but one of the most common responses was to just sit and watch the sea. When asked why they did this and why it was enjoyable, many said that it was because the sea never changed – it was constant and consistent. Perhaps this is what makes test cricket so unique, perhaps why it might endure, and maybe what makes it such a distinctive cultural experience. For me, it made me realize that my grandfather would have known and recognized the same match as I watched. We shared more than the same space, we shared the same experience. His ritual became mine.

As for the match itself, it was far from ordinary. Day one found Leicestershire all out for 141 and, after Kent's response of 533, it was only a matter of time. In the end, Kent won by an innings and 279 runs, ending the match just after tea on the third day. As it turned out, it was rather a historic victory, as it was one of the largest margins of victory for Kent in the club's two-century-plus history. About midway through Day 3 of the match, on another perfect afternoon, my English colleague turned to me and said that, if he could encapsulate England in one picture, it would probably look a little like the St. Lawrence Ground and, in many ways, those three days were the most distinctively English cultural experience I have had. And, although I was happy to have witnessed Kent's triumph for the ages, I was more pleased to have encountered a dual heritage – that of my grandfather, of course, but also that of the country we both love (Figure 5).

Duality of heritage journeys

Graham et al. (2000) argue that, if there is one inherent element to heritage, it is that of dissonance. Lowenthal (1998) also reminds us that heritage is not about fact, but about faith. I know that cricket is not England – that the heritage of England is far more diverse than a sport, and that the spectators at places like the St. Lawrence Ground are not remotely representative of England as a whole. I also do not know for certain that the St. Lawrence Ground held a special place for my grandfather, although I would like to believe that it did. Perhaps if he had lived to talk about it, he would not have remembered his final family trip around Kent or the match vs. Australia. Perhaps even his umpiring days would not have been as romantic as I have imagined they were. In any event, I hardly care for the veracity of this imagined past, but rather the authenticity of the experience. For me, in those three days, I witnessed a distinctive type of English sport culture, with the presence of my grandfather as my guide.

Beyond the connections to family and country, I also found the experience to be timeless, in that it was not confined to a particular time and place. One of the key elements of heritage is that it conflates eras, histories, memories, nostalgias, and impressions. Heritage is often not meant to be precise, which is part of its appeal. However, my experience of timelessness was not an explicit construction. This was not the stuff of pioneer villages, after all, that sell the suspended animation of "ye olde tyme". Rather, it was the impression of a pleasant anachronism. Leaving the ground each day, I felt the jarring sensation of returning to the real world, and each day returning I felt that world disappear. In Thompson's (2012) essay, he felt the real-world creep in as soon as he left the ground as well. Tweeting status updates, using mobile mapping technology to find our way around, using e-mail to catch-up on work – these resume the moment we leave the ground. One observation from three days at the St. Lawrence Ground was that I witnessed a mobile phone used just once during the course of play, and that the spectators within earshot of the conversation gave very disapproving looks to its operator. Reality belongs beyond the boundary, so it would seem.

Heritage can occur almost anywhere, at any time, and be inscribed to anything. Ashworth (2008) reminds us that heritage is not finite; we create it as we need it and discard it when we do not. Heritage also is dynamic; it does not necessarily have to be

Figure 5.   The wicket, looking toward the pavilion at the St. Lawrence Ground, Canterbury. A shared heritage space? I would like to believe that my grandfather may have once umpired at this ground, and may have in fact stood here. (Photo by Gregory Ramshaw)

either collective or personal. However, what this journey taught me was that it is perhaps most powerful when it is both. The St. Lawrence Ground is not a heritage site in a typical sense, though it has a history and hosts a sport that is certainly part of English sporting culture. A tourist watching a match there – or, really, at any county ground – would likely see an authentic glimpse into a type of heritage and, in the case of first class match, perhaps a heritage and tradition under threat. Similarly, a sporting venue is not a typical location for a personal heritage journey though, in my case, standing in the same place as my grandfather was and, perhaps, even umpired was a very powerful heritage experience. Rickly-Boyd (2013) argues that there is a strong connection between the existential state of being and the place and location in which the sense of being takes place, while Timothy and Guelke (2008) reminds us that genealogical searches are often intrinsically geographical. In my case, my connection with my grandfather and my family's heritage was only made possible through the signs and symbols of a more collective – and tangible – cultural location. Each element – the collective and the individual – enhanced the other, and perhaps would have been muted had they not worked in concert. There were times when I was thinking about what my grandfather saw and experienced and, others, when I was simply enjoying a cultural activity. Where one ended and the other began was hardly the point. Rather, experiencing that dual heritage helped me to imagine a past that, perhaps, was invented, but felt altogether true.

Acknowledgements

The research for this paper was made possible by a University Research Project Completion Grant from Clemson University. I would also like to thank Sean Gammon for both his cricket tutorial and comments on the early drafts of this paper.

References

Ashworth, G. J. (2008). Paradigms and paradoxes in planning the past. In M. Smith & L. Onderwater (Eds.), *Selling or telling? Paradoxes in tourism, culture and heritage* (pp. 23–34). Arnhem: ATLAS.

Bale, J. (2003). *Sports geographies* (2nd ed.). London: Routledge.

Brown, L. (2013). Tourism: A catalyst for existential authenticity. *Annals of Tourism Research, 40*(1), 176–190.

Bruner, C. (2005). *Culture on tour: Ethnographies of travel*. Chicago, IL: University of Chicago Press.

Chhabra, D., Healy, R., & Sills, E. (2003). Staged authenticity and heritage tourism. *Annals of Tourism Research, 30*(3), 702–719.

Chronis, A. (2012). Tourists as story-builders: Narrative construction at a heritage museum. *Journal of Travel and Tourism Marketing, 29*(5), 444–459.

Cohen, E. (1988). Authenticity and commoditization in tourism. *Annals of Tourism Research, 15*(3), 371–386.

Cricket Archive. (2012). Kent v. Australians: Australia in the British Isles, 1953. Retrieved June 5, 2012, from http://cricketarchive.com/Archive/Scorecards/20/20869.html

ESPN CricInfo. (2012, April 2). Debate: The future of County Cricket. *The Switch Hit Cricket Show.* Podcast retrieved from http://www.espncricinfo.com/ci/content/multimedia/559568.html

Gammon, S. (2002). Fantasy, nostalgia and the pursuit of what never was. In S. Gammon & J. Kurtzman (Eds.), *Sport tourism: Principals and practice* (pp. 61–72). Eastbourne: Leisure Studies Association.

Gammon, S., & Fear, V. (2007). Stadia tours and the power of backstage. In S. Gammon & G. Ramshaw (Eds.), *Heritage, sport and tourism: Sporting pasts – Tourist futures* (pp. 23–32). London: Routledge.

Graham, B., Ashworth, G. J., & Tunbridge, J. E. (2000). *A geography of heritage: Power, culture & economy*. London: Arnold.

Leiper, N. (1990). Tourist attraction systems. *Annals of Tourism Research, 17,* 367–384.

Lowenthal, D. (1998). *The heritage crusade and the spoils of history*. Cambridge: Cambridge University Press.

MacCannell, D. (1973). Staged authenticity: Arrangements of social space in tourist settings. *American Journal of Sociology, 79*(3), 589–603.

Macdonnell, A. (1935). *England, their England*. London: Macmillian.

MacGregor, R. (2006). Forward. In D. Whitson & R. Gruneau (Eds.), *Artificial ice: Hockey, culture and commerce* (pp. vii–x). Peterborough: Broadview Press.

Pearson, G. (2012, May 23). Kent County Cricket Club see a drop in crowds. *Kent Online*. Retrieved June 19, 2012, from http://www.kentonline.co.uk/kentonline/sport/2012/may/24/kent_crowds.aspx

Poria, Y., Butler, R., & Airey, D. (2001). Clarifying heritage tourism. *Annals of Tourism Research*, *28*(4), 1047–1049.

Poria, Y., Butler, R., & Airey, D. (2003). The core of heritage tourism. *Annals of Tourism Research*, *30*(1), 238–254.

Ramshaw, G., & Gammon, S. (2005). More than just Nostalgia? Exploring the heritage/sport tourism nexus. *Journal of Sport Tourism*, *10*(4), 229–241.

Ramshaw, G., & Gammon, S. (2010). On home ground? Twickenham stadium tours and the construction of sport heritage. *Journal of Heritage Tourism*, *5*(2), 87–102.

Ramshaw, G., & Hinch, T. (2006). Place identity and sport tourism: The case of the heritage classic ice hockey event. *Current Issues in Tourism*, *9*(4&5), 399–418.

Rickly-Boyd, J. M. (2009). The tourist narrative. *Tourist Studies*, *9*(3), 259–280.

Rickly-Boyd, J. M. (2012). 'Through the magic of authentic reproduction': Tourists' perceptions of authenticity in a pioneer village. *Journal of Heritage Tourism*, *7*(2), 127–144.

Rickly-Boyd, J. M. (2013). Existential authenticity: Place matters. *Tourism Geographies*, *15*(4), 680–686. Retrieved February 18, 2013, from http://www.tandfonline.com/doi/abs/10.1080/14616688.2012.762691

Thompson, W. (2012, June 18). "Test of time: In defense of a game that lasts five days". *ESPN: Outside the Lines*. Retrieved June 18, 2012, from http://sports.espn.go.com/espn/eticket/story?page=111225/testcricket

Timothy, D. J. (1997). Tourism and the personal heritage experience. *Annals of Tourism Research*, *24*(3), 751–754.

Timothy, D. J. (2008). Genealogical mobility: Tourism and the search for a personal past. In D. J. Timothy & J. Kay Guelke (Eds.), *Geography and genealogy: Locating personal pasts* (pp. 115–135). Aldershot: Ashgate.

Timothy, D. J. (2011). *Cultural heritage and tourism: An introduction*. Bristol: Channel View Publications.

Timothy, D. J., & Boyd, S. (2003). *Heritage tourism*. London: Prentice Hall.

Timothy, D. J., & Boyd, S. (2006). Heritage tourism in the 21st century: Valued traditions and new perspectives. *Journal of Heritage Tourism*, *1*(1), 1–16.

Timothy, D. J., & Guelke, J. K. (2008). Conclusion: Personal perspectives. In D. J. Timothy & J. K. Guelke (Eds.), *Geography and genealogy: Locating personal pasts* (pp. 175–184). Aldershot: Ashgate.

Wang, N. (1999). Rethinking authenticity in tourism experience. *Annals of Tourism Research*, *26*(2), 349–370.

Index

For Product Safety Concerns and Information please contact our
EU representative GPSR@taylorandfrancis.com Taylor & Francis
Verlag GmbH, Kaufingerstraße 24, 80331 München, Germany